Advance praise for *Talk the Walk*

"With all of Dana Wright-Wasson's experience as well as knowledge of business, she has successfully engaged and captured her reader! This book is a wonderful motivator to 'Never Stop Pushing the Best You Can Be.'"

ROBERTO J. GARCIA, RE-MARKETING SUPPLY SPECIALIST, MARS WRIGLEY CONFECTIONERY

"As Michelle Obama said, 'Success isn't about how much money you make; it's about the difference you make in people's lives.' *Talk the Walk* is a definitive map, written from the heart and full of powerful examples and supported by wonderful graphics. Take this journey with Dana Wright-Wasson and enjoy the abundant returns for you, your teams, organizations, and ideally our world at large."

HELEN-JANE NELSON, FOUNDER & THOUGHT PARTNER, CECARA CONSULTING LIMITED

"*Talk the Walk* is a wonderful trip through the world of leadership, engagement, corporate social responsibility, and so much more related to successful businesses. It's a must-read for those in the business world. Readers will learn how to move themselves and their organizations to even greater success."

SHARON HEFFELFINGER, RETIRED GLOBAL CORPORATE PERSONNEL AND ORGANIZATION MANAGER, MARS, INCORPORATED

"Backed by studies and examples of best practices from real companies, Dana Wright-Wasson shows us the value of recognizing the whole self of the employee—not just the skills a person is hired for."

HEATHER MARTINEZ, VISUAL PRACTITIONER, CHANGE AGENT, COACH

D1212068

"If you're looking for a 'quick fix' for your company's culture, look elsewhere. But if you're looking for deep expertise in how to make your employees feel heard, empowered, and invested in your company's vision, this is the book for you. Dana Wright-Wasson's approachable writing style and many anecdotes make this challenging topic feel accessible and actionable in a way few can."

KYLAH WRIGHT, RETAIL LOYALTY CONSULTANT, LENATI

"Talk the Walk is a brilliant guide to enhancing employee experience. From leadership to culture, systems, and processes, *Talk the Walk* provides practical takeaways for leaders at all levels."

DAVID BURKUS, AUTHOR OF *FRIEND OF A FRIEND* AND *UNDER NEW MANAGEMENT*

"Talk the Walk is timely and readable. Dana Wright-Wasson offers practical insights in how to rethink employee experience in your organization now—emphasizing the role of leadership and communication. Companies that genuinely focus on employee experience are creating a strategic business differentiator to drive results."

NOEL BROWN, SENIOR DIRECTOR OF GLOBAL TALENT ACQUISITION, THERMO FISHER SCIENTIFIC

"Simply genius and perfectly timed. Dana Wright-Wasson advances the emerging conversation of employee experience with a model linked to design thinking. That is already innovative enough, but it's the anecdotes, the case studies, and the bite-sized chapters that make this book both practical and a delight to read for leaders of any kind of organization."

JESSE FEWELL, AUTHOR OF *CAN YOU HEAR ME NOW?*

"Dana Wright-Wasson is brilliant at creating the most inspiring experience for groups of all sizes. *Talk the Walk* is a very entertaining and informative read with a no-nonsense and easy-to-apply tone that can be successfully used by anyone who wants to positively impact the engagement experience."

TAMI MAJER, HEAD OF HR, DANONE NORTH AMERICA

"Put down whatever else you're reading right now and buy this book. *Talk the Walk* is so much more than a book about world-class employee experience. It contains the wisdom from decades of work helping organizations become their best. Reading it was like taking a graduate-level course in what it takes to create and run a healthy, sustainable organization. Dana Wright-Wasson's style is accessible, even neighborly, yet unquestionably learned. In considering employee experience through a variety of lenses, Dana covers organizational culture, leadership, people practices, and more. What's more, she backs it all up with relevant stories from real organizations reflecting the struggles and choices of living, breathing folks like you and me. Whether you're a manager, an executive, running a line in a factory, or sitting in an office, you will find *Talk the Walk* an irreplaceable resource on your journey to making your work and workplace more powerful and meaningful."

CARLOS VALDES-DAPENA, PRINCIPAL, CORPORATE COLLABORATION RESOURCES, LLC, AND AUTHOR OF *LESSONS FROM MARS*

"Employee engagement, leadership, and culture are all well-worn topics that you've probably read a dozen books about. Each. But you need to read Dana Wright-Wasson's outstanding book *Talk the Walk* because it's better than most books on any of those topics. Dana shows you the subtle (and not so subtle) interconnections between your efforts in these areas—and how to finally dial in the unique combination that will work and last for your specific organization to transform your results. Buy a copy for everyone on your team and watch what happens."

DAVID NEWMAN, AUTHOR OF *DO IT! MARKETING* AND *DO IT! SPEAKING*

"Getting the most out of yourself and your team is a daunting task. We're told that workers find themselves increasingly disengaged from their jobs, their colleagues, and even their authentic selves. In this book, Dana Wright-Wasson provides a guide to a powerful collection of frameworks you can leverage to increase knowledge of yourself and enhance engagement within your team."

LUKE HOHMANN, FOUNDER AND CEO, CONTENEO

"Dana Wright-Wasson's book is rich with tips, stories, quotations, and anecdotes that will undoubtedly play an important and instructive role in shifting the conversation about what 'engagement' means. Dana's deep experience in the field, along with her comprehensive inquiry into leading practices, help us to reveal the humane nature of engagement. Dana's wisdom is simple but not simplistic: start conversations, create the space for stories to happen, and listen."

ANTHONY WEEKS, PUBLIC LISTENER AND VISUAL STORYTELLER

TALK THE WALK

Here's to
Having Conversations
that Matter!

DANA WRIGHT-WASSON

FOUNDER, THE WORK HAPPY PROJECT

TALK

– THE –

WALK

Designing a Clear Path to a
World Class Employee Experience

Page Two Books
www.pagetwobooks.com
Cover design by Taysia Louie
Cover illustrations by Dana Wright-Wasson
Interior design by Taysia Louie
Interior illustrations by Marianne Rodgers

www.take-action.com

Also by Dana Wright-Wasson:

*We've Got to START Meeting Like This! Creating Inspiring Meetings,
Conferences and Events* (2013)

To Meet or NOT to Meet? 10 Tips for Practically Perfect Meetings (2015)

To my mom, who demonstrated you can be intelligent, curious and kind, and my dad, who taught me the importance of always challenging yourself

Contents

Conscious Leadership Attributes
Courageous Leadership
Building Trust Through Purpose
Get to Know Your People
How to Become a Conscious Leader
Strive to Become Your Best Self

Leaders Who Listen
How to Lead with Your Ears
Reducing Misconceptions: Contact Hypothesis
Shared Humanity
Really Seeing People
How to Listen Like a Leader
One-on-One Communication
Words Matter
Design Thinking and Leadership

Learning to Manage Busy-ness
Meetings Can Create Engagement
Control Yourself

Contributing to the Community
Triple Bottom Line

PART FOUR: PROCESSES THAT WELCOME EMPLOYEES

Hiring for Attitude
Hire Slowly. Fire Quickly.
Getting the Right People Is Up to You

Make a Great First Impression

PART FIVE: PROCESSES THAT ENHANCE
THE EMPLOYEE EXPERIENCE

PART SIX: PRACTICAL APPLICATIONS

    Step 1: Scoping
    Step 2: Conducting Listening Sessions
    Step 3: Employee Action Planning
    Step 4: Leadership Action Planning
    Step 5: Sharing the Work
    Step 6: Work-Out Sessions

Foreword

By Tom Nerviano

I N SPRING 2013, the senior supply chain leader at our company suggested that I connect with Dana Wright-Wasson, who had developed an "employee engagement" process that he'd seen result in very positive outcomes at another global company. He preferred Dana's approach to our home-grown program. Though we had pride of ownership for our methodology, as we had invested a great deal of energy and resources over the past five years, it didn't take a political genius to agree to try out Dana's process and compare it with our own.

So, off our band of HR professionals went to Kentucky to learn the process and pilot this new approach at a factory. Afterward, our team would make an objective assessment of both approaches and recommend the way forward. It was tough, but we had to acknowledge that Dana had a much better design. We humbly retired our program and delivered Dana's employee experience program across all of our North American sites.

With Dana's guidance, we involved everyone at each site in helping to identify the issues or circumstances that were causing a subset of employees at all levels to be disengaged. Previously, we'd relied on the management team to make the necessary changes and solve the big problems—clearly a design flaw. Using this new process, we harnessed the power of 100 per cent to define work streams, achieve higher employee engagement, and re-engage the disengaged.

Over time, our HR community grew by honing our facilitation skills, immersing ourselves in the current thinking by reading books and articles, and acquiring a more personal appreciation for the power of engagement and employee experience. We truly came together as a team and made a difference in the working lives of employees across the supply chain network. That's how valuable Dana's process is for employees at all levels. And as you would expect, we were most successful when site leaders got on board. For any process or methodology to have a lasting impact, leaders have to believe that a positive and healthy employee experience will yield a competitive advantage and contribute to the long-term viability of the organization.

I have great respect for Dana, her deep knowledge of employee experience, and the energy and passion she brings to her clients and her work. In this book, Dana shares the wisdom from her life experiences, wide-ranging reading, and engagement workshops. She systematically guides the reader through the elements of the employee experience while providing examples from large and small organizations, as well as practical insights. Read this book cover to cover and keep it nearby as your go-to employee experience reference.

TOM NERVIANO worked at Unilever NA for over thirty-three years, and as an HR director or leader partnered with supply chain, customer development, and marketing.

Making a Difference:
The Starfish Story

Original story by Loren Eisley

AN OLD MAN had a habit of early morning walks on the beach. One day, after a storm, he saw a human figure in the distance moving like a dancer. As he came closer he saw that it was a young woman and she was not dancing but was reaching down to the sand, picking up starfish one at a time and very gently throwing them into the ocean.

"Young lady," he asked, "Why are you throwing starfish into the ocean?"

"The sun is up, and the tide is going out, and if I do not throw them in they will die," she said.

"But young lady, do you not realize that there are miles and miles of beach and starfish all along it? You cannot possibly make a difference."

The young woman listened politely, paused, and then bent down, picked up another starfish, and threw it into the sea, past the breaking waves, and said, "It made a difference for that one."

Introduction

I WAS FIRST EXPOSED to the concept of customer experience (CX) when I worked with a company that sold diabetes meters. Walking through a customer lifecycle with their product was eye-opening. Customer experience asks that we look at every aspect of how a product could be experienced by a customer, from the first phone call or internet search to follow-up help calls and everything in between. Type 1 diabetes patients are typically children. Considering how children and families are affected by the disease helped the company be compassionate and sympathetic to their challenges on a daily and lifetime basis.

It was a revelation when companies began to think of their customers as they designed and marketed their products. The world of marketing has been focused on customer experience/the voice of the customer for years, looking through customers' eyes to determine what happens at every stage of their journey for a product or service. The idea of putting the customer first, thinking through their eyes, made companies consider their wants, needs, and desires. In fact, Amazon dedicates an empty chair in every meeting to keep their customer top of mind. According to Gartner, today more than 90 per cent of businesses compete primarily on the basis of customer experience.

When it comes to employees, the focus has shifted from satisfaction surveys to engagement surveys to measure the internal health of their employees, often referred to as "human resources" or "talent." The majority of companies have been doing employee engagement surveys for the better part of two decades now; sadly, little is changing for employees. Foosball tables and beanbag chairs are fun but not ways to create engagement. Why has all the money spent on surveys, books on the topic, and training courses not moved the needle and created vast improvements?

The answer seems clear as day.

An engagement survey, in fact *any* type of survey, is a lagging indicator, not a leading indicator. In other words, these surveys measure the outcomes, the results of what the company is doing (or not doing), rather than actually driving employee engagement.

Instead, the focus really needs to be on the things that create engagement, looking at the leading indicators. These factors are what create the experience an employee has with a company. So like CX, we are now looking at employee experience, thinking of the employee as a very important customer.

This took me a long time to figure out. I, too, was caught up in trying to take the results of a survey and work backwards to resolve the issues. What was getting in the way of full engagement? What issues were causing people to be disengaged? This was clearly reactive problem-solving after the fact, not proactive problem-finding beforehand.

In other words, we've been chasing ambulances. In fact, we've been throwing billions of dollars at the ambulances as they whiz by.

It's funny, because in my personal life I'm all about preventative medicine. I believe strongly in health care, rather than sick care. Instead of taking care of the issues that arise after I'm already sick, how can I focus on making myself as healthy as possible and use data to make improvements and adjustments?

I do the same thing with organizations, applying both my education in organization development and my many years of experience in culture transformation, leadership, and engagement. In this book, I will suggest ways that leaders across any organization can look at the things that contribute to a great experience for employees, from the very first time they interact with the organization in the hiring process to the very last day they work as an employee.

So, How Would I Define Employee Experience (EX)?

For me, employee experience is everything that's connected with an employee's interaction with the company. It's about the day-to-day experiences they have with the work environment, the culture, and leaders in the organization. It's about the values that are demonstrated by everyone in the organization. It's about the clear purpose that the organization is delivering to the world. It's about a leadership focus on people skills that help draw out the best in everyone who works there.

It's not about fun work environments for the sake of fun—the beanbag chairs and free food are nice, but they alone don't create a great employee experience. It's not about branding, because what you may tell potential employees on the outside doesn't matter if your Glassdoor reviews, done by existing employees, tell a different story. And again, it's not to be confused with employee engagement, which is the goal instead of all the things that get you there.

Employee experience requires an honest, thorough look at the organization's culture: what are the obvious and not-so-obvious ways that the values and behaviors are supporting or sabotaging success? And how are leaders helping and supporting employees to grow, explore, and innovate? All three of these factors—processes, culture, and leadership—are needed to create a thriving employee experience.

It would be easy to say all of this falls in the lap of Human Resources (HR); after all, HR is responsible for some of the key people processes, like hiring, firing, and managing performance appraisals. HR can coach the senior leaders to understand their role in leading the organization, but they can only do so much. The concept of EX requires much more than what HR alone can do.

Why Is It Important to Get It Right?

One thing that's clear is the workplace is rapidly changing. With the influx of Millennials, employers are scrambling to figure out what makes this new generation tick. And they should: this is one of the largest generations in the last century to join the workforce, and they have very different ideas than their parents or grandparents for what makes a great career. They are, by and large, educated, tech-savvy, and not willing to sacrifice their whole life for their job. They are interested in contributing to their community and they want, sometimes demand, balance.

With technology and social media, these digital natives can easily tell which organizations align with their values and purpose, just by looking online. Information is so easily shared internally that smart companies try to stay on top of things before they turn into issues, but it's harder than ever to do this.

Our Unique Approach to Employee Experience

For years, I've set up my engagement approach to be experiential and interactive. I don't rely on surveys for information, but actually talk to people to find out how they experience the organization day to day. I work with the organization's leaders to make sure they have the skills and knowledge to really help and engage people in their work and in their growth. My conversational approach is visual, in that I capture the information that employees share in real time, and make sure it's true to what they mean. And then I involve both leaders and employees in the solutions, because they know best what will create a better place to work. Only by working together can everyone create an amazing, meaningful employee experience.

I want reading this book to be a fun and engaging experience. So, I've put in lots of examples, lots of inspirational and relevant quotes, tips and lists, and playful illustrations. You can read in order or skip around to the chapters that interest you. I promise it's all good reading. And you'll be glad you put in the time to learn new things. My hope is you'll be inspired to create some great experiences of your own, and keep the conversation going in your organization. After all, the hallmark of a great leader, at any level, is exhibiting the values of the company through their daily behavior, right down to their listening and speaking style. Values grow and evolve. You can't just post the values on a bulletin board somewhere and hope that employees walk the walk; instead, you have to show them how to talk the walk.

1

Defining
Employee
Experience

1

It's All About
the Experience

KNOW NONE OF us wants to believe the future of work is going to be much different from the past. Despite the exclamation of how Millennials are changing the workplace, and how technology is changing at such a rapid rate, the facts that drive many of us to work are still the same: we need to get paid so we have money for somewhere to live, for food, for transportation, and for kids and pets. And then, we also want money for extra things and activities that bring joy and fulfillment to our lives, be it decorating items, nice clothes, or travel and adventure. I know—I stick by this view myself.

However, what those of us in the middle to later end of our careers can't understand is what it's actually like to grow up as a digital native: to always have information at your fingertips. And that *does* change the world and the way we work. And technology *does* have a huge impact on how things get done; because we can't always get it right the first time, we have to stumble and make mistakes in the mix of when digital is the right answer and when tasks must be done by a human. Take customer service voice prompts. I would propose many

"Success is not the key to happiness. Happiness is the key to success. If you have what you're doing, you will be successful."

ALBERT SCHWEITZER

companies still don't have this right: my experience is that the bot on the other end of the phone can't service my needs, yet I can't reach a human to resolve a problem. Or a company that is so web-based that their Frequently Asked Questions (FAQs) don't answer *my* question, but there's no other way to reach someone at the company.

So what does the future of work hold for us, and why does getting the employee experience right matter so much?

First, work in the future is going to be a combination of technology and humans; in fact, it's already here and will just increase. Smart companies will tell you that we are in a mindset shift from "doing digital" to "being digital"—all companies are or will be digital in the next few years. The 2017 Deloitte Global Human Capital Trends cites the topic of "organization design" to be number one on corporate leaders' minds—this was barely talked about when I got my degree in organization development twenty years ago. Things like agile teams, networked roles, and the ability to work flexibly will be key to success.

The fast-paced changes in technology mean that people can't stop learning when they leave a formal institution; instead, they make learning new skills and new thinking just part of life. Jobs in the future will be things technology can't do: focused more on creative, social, soft skills. So, work environments have to foster and reward continuous learning and sharing knowledge.

> *"Technology is nothing. What's important is that you have a faith in people, that they're basically good and smart, and if you give them tools, they'll do wonderful things with them."* STEVE JOBS

For as long as I can remember, my clients have talked about a "war on talent." This need has only become more important as technology continues to evolve. Social media sites like LinkedIn and Glassdoor make it very easy for potential employees to know a lot about a company; if they have talent and a smidgen of confidence, they can really be selective of where they want to work.

This is where the topic of employee experience comes in. If a company isn't highly rated or considered a good place to work, it becomes hard to attract and retain the talent that's required to suc-ceed. And, with highly sought skills, employees want to be with companies that are growing, well-respected, and fun places to work. Companies have to make sure that the experience is well thought out from start to finish. This requires moving from thinking about employees as expendable resources to, instead, thinking of them as highly valued talent, and that it's important to understand their needs. Companies must continuously involve employees in gathering ideas for improvement, and then co-create a truly great experience— from onboarding to recognition and rewards.

The thinking around employee experience also includes thinking about the organization's leadership: leading and inspiring people has become a critical skillset for organizations. Successful leaders also have to embrace the concept of continuous learning for two reasons. One, because the way they were led will generally not be the way they will successfully lead others. And two, the focus on skills like empathy and humbleness will be so important because there won't be a way to know everything with changes happening both rapidly and all the time; a team approach is the only way to effectively get things done.

Engagement Is a Feeling, Not a Number

Employee engagement has become one of the most talked-about top-ics for businesses from Gallup to the *Harvard Business Review*, and yet very few people can give a simple and concise definition of what exactly it is. There are statistics that say anywhere from 65 per cent to 85 per cent of workers globally are not engaged and that this costs companies in the United States alone $550 billion a year. Gallup employee engagement research indicates that a disengaged employee can cost a company up to 34 per cent of their annual salary. But none of that helps understand what engagement actually is, what it does, or how to define and explain it.

While I've worked in this space for over ten years, I'm not sure I can give a simple definition either, because so much of it is a feeling.

It is the feeling that comes from employee experience. Engagement is often thought of as what surveys measure: a number that can be tracked. I don't believe that something so complex and so much a part of the texture and feel of an organization can be explained with a number. There is so much more to it than that. In fact, I would say that there is more said in the white space between the questions in any survey, that the number itself is practically useless to an organization except as a tracking device.

Engagement is a feeling. It's something you know immediately when you walk through the door of any company or organization, large or small. For example, when I walk into a well-known department chain store as a customer, I can tell there is a lack of employee engagement: the merchandise is cluttered, the bathrooms are dirty and old, and when I manage to find a salesperson, they're not very interested in helping me. I have been working for more than ten years to help companies raise their engagement scores, their "number," and I know what an engaged place feels like. This may sound nebulous to you, hard to put your finger on. But by the end of this section, after introducing you to how to define and think about engagement, you will be able to clearly know when it is there and when it isn't, too.

> *"What you do speaks so loudly that I cannot hear what you say."*
> RALPH WALDO EMERSON

Engagement is when people are really proud to talk about their company. They gush about the way their company runs, about its transparency, about how rigorous the hiring is, and about how good the internal processes are. They also share the tangible things, like when I visited Facebook in Menlo Park. As an employee walked me around campus, he pointed out the onsite dry cleaning, the bicycle repair shop, the various free food kiosks. He proudly told me the area where we were walking was designed by the same architect who designed Main Street at Disneyland, with its scaled-down storefronts.

Engagement is when the company culture is obvious from the moment you walk through the door, in a consistent, real way. Lenati is a small marketing and sales strategy consulting firm headquartered in Seattle. Their corporate culture is one of deep employee engagement where they focus on development and growth. During my visit to Lenati, it was clear that engagement is embedded in everything they do: how they communicate, the energy of the office, and how their employees were excited and inspired to tell me about their work. I will be using them as an example throughout the book for the simple reason that they have consciously created a successful employee experience and were able to articulate the experience very clearly.

Engagement is when employees know they are more than cogs in a wheel: their personal mission aligns with what they understand as the company's purpose. In Gallup's engagement survey, they ask, "Do you have a best friend at work?" Often people feel strange about that question. It somehow hits close to the issue: are you cared about and do you feel attached to the work you do and the people with whom you do it? But it's hard to answer that in a survey. There is too much nuance and the real answer lies in the white space around the question.

Engagement is when employees feel recognized for the work they do and are enabled to develop so they can continue to improve. Recognition is key, whether it is being acknowledged by simple thank-yous, being noticed and called out in a special way, being asked to teach others, being given a gift card or a parking space—it all helps employees feel seen. Learning, which is crucial to engagement, can happen in both official and casual ways.

Experience and Engagement

Engagement, when you look at it as a way to talk about employee experience, is everything a person encounters from the moment they first interact with a company to the moment they say their goodbyes as they leave their job. It puts engagement in a new light because it means that everything you do, and everything that touches employees, can improve what they experience.

These are all part of the feeling of engagement, which by the end of this section, you will be able to pick up yourself; by the end of the book, you will have lots of ideas of things to try. But let's get more specific about the definition of engagement.

A longer list of definitions includes:

- Enjoying spending time at work and being motivated to come to work.
- Putting out your best effort every day.
- Knowing you have an impact, that what you do matters and makes a difference.
- Having a passion for what you do.
- Feeling part of a family.
- Feeling good about yourself at the end of the day.
- Enjoying what you're doing.
- Feeling like a necessary part of the organization.

No workplace is perfect and no one loves every aspect of their job all the time. Let's be clear about that. There are parts of every work situation that will be far from perfect. We're not creating utopia, just a place where work gets done well and people are fulfilled by what they do and feel important to how it gets done.

> *"Treat employees like they make a difference and they will."*
> JIM GOODNIGHT, CEO, SAS

Not everyone is going to feel this way, even in one of the organizations called out as highly engaged. Even in a very healthy environment there will be a range of engagement. Here we are talking about moving more people into higher engagement in every company, so let's look at how they typically fall out across a spectrum of engagement.

Typically, employee engagement divides people into three categories:

Engaged and Inspired—or as Jennifer Blackmon, Corporate Director of Culture Transformation at the Ritz-Carlton, refers to them, "superstars—engaged and committed," which is about 30 per cent of an organization.

Disengaged—those who are there, present, and do what's expected but nothing more; about 50 per cent of an organization.

Actively Disengaged—the "cancer of an organization," people who act like prisoners in organizations and are not only negative but are actively, even if unconsciously, trying to recruit others to be negative as well. They represent about 20 per cent of an organization.

According to Gallup, we have three natural desires of our work. The first is to be treated as a person, not a number or an "asset." The second is to feel appreciated and valued. The third is to feel that one's contributions make a difference. So that is another way to assess whether an organization feels engaged.

In other words, businesses have two options: make good hiring decisions, treat people well and give them freedom, and they will be productive and happy; or treat people badly, let the good ones leave and fire others, get new people and start over, and then find yourself in a vicious, negative cycle. The US Department of Labor estimates that, on average, it costs one-third of a new hire's annual salary to replace an employee who has left the company. So there's a financial advantage to figuring this out.

Engagement Is Everyone's Thing

I've often heard people refer to engagement as an "HR thing," which is most definitely not the case. There is no way one function or one group of people can change engagement for an entire company. This belief is just a trick of history. Back when measuring began in the 1940s, organizations measured whether employees were "satisfied" or not at work. HR owned the results of these satisfaction surveys and tried to implement programs that would help create more overall satisfaction at work. Things progressed this way for decades; then, in the late '90s, measuring employee engagement gained popularity, more research was done, and company leaders wanted to know how invested their employees were in the company and in their work.

To change the experience and culture of an organization, you need to have day-to-day contact with employees. The people who have that kind of contact are managers, not HR. Therefore, the results of these engagement surveys became the responsibility of the managers. HR may have had some ideas about how to launch programs, which may or may not have been effective; but you can bet that managers, who generally had no idea how to create better workplaces, were at a loss as to how to change the satisfaction levels of their direct reports. They just knew how to manage, not lead people. So, they were left to figure it out; they were fired if they did not get those numbers up. That practice exists implicitly or explicitly in many companies today. Get those numbers up or you'll be looking for another job.

Engagement really is that important, but it's way too important to leave people to figure it out for themselves. You end up with horror stories like I've heard, where people get big fancy dinners right before the engagement surveys go out or are pressured to report better scores. Engagement is too important to be left to surveys that allow for those tactics.

And yet it's very important to pay attention to engagement, especially the actively disengaged. These people, who comprise 20 per cent of a business's employee population, drain the organization:

they monopolize the manager's time, create more on-the-job accidents, create more quality defects, contribute to shrinkage (theft), take more sick time, and ultimately quit or cause the high-performing people to quit.

You can generally recognize an engaged person right away. Pay attention to your interactions with people and assess whether after the encounter you have more or less energy. People who energize you are generally more effective, more innovative, and have better performance overall.

Engaged employees are heaters: they give off energy, you want to be around them. They help your organization feel good. I had a client who had an employee also named Dana. Among many things, she worked very hard to organize her leadership team's annual conference. She was a joy to be around, and I looked forward to interacting with her. Our work was so successful and playful that we began to call each other "Thing One" and "Thing Two" from Dr. Seuss. The names stuck and the sense of play expanded to include everyone helping to put on the meeting. That is a heater experience.

Disengagement feels just the opposite. I once facilitated a meeting where the leader kept interrupting people as they spoke and set a negative tone in the room that made me, and probably everyone else, want to run out the door. I had the liberty to just say no to future work, but as I left I worried about the people who worked with her, and downstream from her, and how unlikely they were to ever brag about their job or their work in a happy, healthy way.

It goes almost without saying that engagement is a good thing. We want to create warm, heater spaces and moments and feelings in our companies. We want people to do more work than asked, brag about the place they work, create the same feelings in the people they see every day, and make the business we do successful while they make themselves happy. We want to have employees who do this for each other. And we want to support them. So how do we do that, and what are the common beliefs we need to step over to get to real engagement? If this concept of engagement is so universally good, why isn't everyone engaged?

2

Surveys Measure What, Exactly?

Emphasizing Numbers Over People

We're not creating a better employee experience or realizing better engagement primarily because we misunderstand it. We don't know how to assess it when we see it (or don't see it) and create problems because we want it to be measurable as a number, not a feeling. We make engagement both more difficult and less successful because we are trying to treat it the same way we treat statistics, and people are simply not quantifiable.

One way we miss the forest for the trees in engagement is that we pay too much attention to survey results. Leaders tend to focus too much on the percentages, the numbers, and treat them as moveable parts. They don't think about the fact that sometimes the numbers represent people who are unhappy or a culture that needs to change. What leaders think instead is *this percentage needs to go up by 10 per cent*. And suddenly the situation is worse. People who had previously not been heard told the truth and asked for help through the survey, and they are now being ignored.

> "Survey says Americans are getting tired of surveys"
>
> **NEWSPAPER HEADLINE**

Employees end up fearing surveys because nothing positive happens; often, something negative happens. Managers begin to fear consequences if their numbers are not high enough. This voluntary survey begins to take on a fear factor. Consultant Patrick Marr, of UK-based Leading Edge, compared engagement surveys to a bathroom scale. The survey may be a measure of output, like weighing oneself and seeing a number. But the number itself is not engagement, and it doesn't really help anyone to know what input created that number or what to do to improve the number.

When the survey numbers are the main focus, two problems occur. One we call a "Steak and Cake" problem, where people are bribed, or threatened, in order to change the survey results. When it is survey time, managers organize things like steak lunches with cake for dessert, in the hopes that this will help employees see the management in a good light and give them high marks, raising the numbers on the survey.

The other problem is simply the lack of human interaction. With technology, we are rapidly losing so much human connection in society. Surveys miss the nuance of how people think and feel and what motivates them. You have no idea what their numerical answers really mean.

Remember, surveys become part of employee experience and they become something the employee has to endure. If you want a positive experience for your employees, you need to find a better way to ascertain what they need.

Without human interaction, it's difficult to understand what's behind the numbers you receive. How we respond to any survey can vary day to day based on what we are experiencing at that time. It's just hard to tell if it's a momentary issue, an entrenched issue, and even which issue caused the resulting numbers.

Annual surveys also suffer from the inevitable lag time between the administration of the survey and the availability of results, sometimes as much as three to four months. A lot can change in that time! What was happening at the time the survey was given? Sometimes there was a layoff, or a significant person left the organization. Other happenings, like big project deadlines or organizational changes, can affect people's mindsets. It can be hard to make the link between the survey results based on factors that existed at the time and the current circumstances.

For me, engagement surveys are like annual performance appraisals: everyone dreads them, and often nothing useful comes from the amount of effort that went into them. And yet, usually, people do want useful feedback on how they are doing so they can make changes and improve—just not twelve months of feedback all at one time.

The survey may lead to more work but not necessarily anything that changes how employees feel about their work. Managers are fearful of what will come out of surveys and aren't really open or prepared to hear the feedback. It can end up feeling painful and personal.

These are just some of the reasons that I'm not a fan of surveys. I do believe it is crucial to understand how people feel about their work. Without a doubt, it is possible to assess and even change how they feel. I have been there with clients as they do it.

Here's the bottom line on surveys for me:
It's not about the numbers.
It's not about the bar graphs.
It's not about the score.
And by the time you see it, it's probably old news.

If We Knew What to Do, We'd Have Done It Already

If leaders, managers of people, knew what to do to create a better experience for their employees, they would've done it already. Using the scale analogy again, they would've changed their diet or exercised more. But instead, they're sometimes victims of the survey themselves and are handed data that they're supposed to "fix." This causes leaders to feel like the survey is a manager-rating tool.

The result? Managers take one of three approaches. First, try to be extra nice to their team in the hopes that they can emotionally bribe them to get a better score. Second, seek revenge, looking for the culprit(s) who may have given them a bad score and weed them out or punish them. As you can imagine, neither of these approaches is really productive in changing the engagement of their team.

The third approach, which I highly recommend and which this book is about, is to use the data as a springboard for conversations. What story is the data telling you? How do the previous scores relate to the current scores? As with performance appraisals, the data allows you to shift to an ongoing series of dialogues and conversations about what the team is doing well and where it can improve. The data can also inform the leader how they can better support and enable their team.

Getting feedback quickly can generate better conversations and more engagement. For example, Amazon uses a pulse survey system called Connections, which sends out a daily survey to employees. Questions include things like training opportunities, job satisfaction, and leadership. The confidential responses are sent to a centralized

Amazon team to aggregate and then share a daily report with the company's leadership. At eBay, engagement surveys, which take three minutes to complete, are run three times a year and the results are available immediately. They also administer pulse surveys twice in the first ninety days for new hires.

If you're asking fewer questions in gamified ways, then the concept of an engagement survey may be less demanding to your employees. And if it leads to conversation and continuous improvement of the employee experience, even better.

By involving the team in the conversation about both the data and ways to create more engagement, you get them involved in identifying focus areas and then finding solutions. People want to be heard, not quantified. If you actually want to understand people, you have to talk to them.

Old school. Conversations. Listening.

It's the way you get information that matters, and you also raise engagement by doing it.

Do we have a problem with our employees' experience at work? It may be the most important question leaders can ask. Engagement has a feel, it is a palpable part of the organization, it exists everywhere, and it's of vital importance to the bottom line. So how do you find out?

3

How Do You Know You Have Engagement?

If Not a Survey, Then What?

MARS In one of my first engagement sessions at Mars, Incorporated, I was working with two of my favorite internal change agents, Jen Schulte and Jim Brodie. We were called in to this particular site because, according to their engagement scores, they were considered "chronic underperformers," meaning their office's scores just wouldn't go up despite having the same training and same types of jobs as other locations around the world. Jen, as Global Engagement Director, said she overheard one of the senior leaders say, "These associates are not engageable!" As Jen remembers, "When I heard this, I took it as a challenge to prove him wrong, so I pulled my resources together to find out what the real issues were." Happily, I was one of those resources.

"Stay away from negative people. They have a problem for every solution."

ALBERT EINSTEIN

Our two-day session was held in a remote location called Johnston Woods, a rural area of Tennessee. Joining us were seventeen unhappy associates, representing the rest of the workforce. These associates were selected because they were known to be vocal about the key issues impacting site performance. We came in and said to them, "Talk to us." While it took some effort to build trust, they began to talk openly with us, sharing their frustrations and concerns.

However, even though we had been open to listen to them, they were unconvinced that "management" would listen or do anything. At the end of Day One, Jim said to the group, "Listen, if you really don't think anything can or will change, we don't want to waste your time or ours. So we'll be here tomorrow morning, and if you believe we can help create change, then come and join us. The choice is yours." When we arrived the next day, we were uncertain what would happen. But slowly, people started showing up, until every single person was there! And more importantly, they showed up with an attitude of wanting to make a difference.

At one point, one of the associates said, "You know, we work 24/7, nights and weekends. We depend on the vending machines in the breakroom for food. But lots of times, they are completely empty. Here we are in the middle of nowhere and we have no access to food or something to drink. Please help us."

When the site leader and the HR head came in, they listened to what the associates presented, asking thoughtful questions. They realized there were several issues that would take a lot of work. But there were also issues, like the food issue, that were simple to solve and would create belief and trust immediately.

Upon hearing the issues with food, the site leader said, "We can solve that right away." And he followed up and resolved it the very next week.

Let me repeat that. The manager heard the problem, and it was pretty simple to address. He fixed it. And within a week his associates started to see follow-through on his commitment. More than that, they started to believe management cared about them.

It was one of those life-changing moments when we realized people are struggling at work for legitimate reasons, and a survey could not possibly get to the root of the problem because a survey is not a means of communication. These poor people could have had food available a long time ago if someone had bothered to ask them the right questions. But "Do you have reliable access to food?" is not a question on any engagement survey. This situation stuck in my mind because it was so easy to solve.

In the old days, companies had a relationship with their employees with an assumed contract. An employee could expect that if you showed up and did your job, you would move up the corporate ladder, receive benefits and pay increases to keep up with the cost of living, and then a good pension when you retired. This expectation was crushed when IBM had their first massive layoffs in the 1980s and has continued with companies ever since.

Today's norm seems to be that companies take care of their own needs and employees take care of theirs, with no expected loyalty on either side. In times of economic slowdown, I've seen companies treat employees as expendable overhead, even to the point of hearing managers say to employees, "If you don't like it, then there's the door."

I've always felt the attitude of considering employees as expendable is very short-sighted, because when the economy turns around and job options open up again (and so far it always has), employees will remember these words and the people who said them. Two things happen: one, the empowered and confident employees take their skills and go somewhere they are appreciated; two, many who don't leave, mostly because they don't feel like they have options, end up becoming actively disengaged. Neither is a great option for the company. People, especially good people, will disappear if we don't take care of them.

In one focus group I led, someone described an experience of a co-worker being injured very seriously on the job. As they were being carried out to an ambulance, their manager was following along saying, "You can't use sick days for this." Even though I was there to help the company improve their employee engagement (and I knew it was going to improve), when I heard that story, I was stunned.

How could there be a leader anywhere who would say such a horrible thing to their employee? When, through our process, we shared it with the management team, they were also horrified and yet it helped the leaders to understand why people had become disengaged in their work environment.

A Gallup poll of more than one million employed US workers concluded that the number one reason people quit their jobs was an ineffective manager or immediate supervisor. So, the manager above might be a very exaggerated example (though true) but it's instructive.

One of my favorite management quotes is a good summary of this principle: "People join companies and leave managers."

What Works?

What works is creating and sustaining a culture of accountability and trust. There needs to be the assumption of responsibility on both sides. In the instance of the person told not to use sick leave, the company needed to care for the employee; in return, the company would have an employee who uses fewer sick days. One of the things engagement surveys have told us that's useful is that if people care and are engaged, you don't need to worry about sick leave because they use less of it anyway. The use of sick days is not something I think is a great measure of success, but it illustrates the principle that if people are engaged, all other outcomes tend to improve.

> *"People leave because of an attitude of indifference."*
> JENNIFER BLACKMON, CORPORATE DIRECTOR OF CULTURE TRANSFORMATION, RITZ-CARLTON

If leaders and managers are the number one reason why people leave a job, then it stands to reason they could also be a reason to stay. Leaders know where to focus their energy. Consider this pyramid of focus areas. Effective leaders focus on the top two rows:

We will talk in later chapters about vision and planning, but here it is important to say that if leaders are leading with great vision, plans are widely understood, and people feel their work is valued and understand how it's connected to the larger plan, then engagement goes up.

There are generational differences in how long people want to stay at a single job or employer. So even longevity in a company can't be considered the final metric for a successful employee experience. Baby Boomers and Gen X employees often saw their parents stay with companies throughout their career, but didn't have any expectation that their careers would be the same. The newest and most talked-about generations, Millennials and Gen Z, have different demands—wanting to have both their own work and the company's work make a difference and be socially responsible. They expect fluidity in their career and aren't afraid to try things and move around. They have a hunger for meaning and lifelong learning. So don't expect them to stay in one place, no matter how great the experience is.

"The only way to do great work is to love what you do. If you haven't found it yet, keep looking. Don't settle." STEVE JOBS

Engagement is going to look different to different people, but it will feel the same when a company has it. When I started working, I remember working with people who had been at the company for fifteen, twenty, even twenty-five years. I remember the impact this had on me, because I set a five-year goal for myself. I needed to be out of there in five years or I would get more attached to the things that created security, like the benefits; I would start to care less about the work, growing, and taking risks. I met my goal and I moved on.

My Millennial daughter started her career recently and there was no assumption that she would be there for any set number of years. The mindset of her generation is totally different. She is trying to develop a meaningful career, not focused on getting retirement benefits. And we need to keep all these differences in mind when we talk to people about engagement. Showing up for twenty-five years is not enough and it is not engagement; in fact, it's one of my pet peeves when organizations give longevity awards or awards for perfect attendance. That is not engagement. You can do that and hate your job. Engagement has to focus on more than showing up.

Work and Well-Being

Gallup and others have been able to make a strong link between work and work's health impacts. It's not surprising, given how much time we spend at work, the impact that work has on our physical and mental health. Physical labor has had much more attention put on it, with ergonomics related to lifting and moving things, as well as sitting at desks. But the emotional drains of stressful workplaces and the links to both physical and mental ailments are only beginning to be understood.

Research backs me up. Engagement and well-being are linked and have an impact on you and the people you work with and for. Workplace well-being also has an impact on both your family and your community. When you're happy at work, it ripples out to your personal life, family life, and community. Positive or negative, it impacts how you interact with the world, starting with yourself and your physical well-being. This well-being factor is not something every company understands but should.

Companies want to have employees who feel like owners, not renters. Renters don't want to invest because, to them, it's someone else's job to do that and they are not committed for the long haul. Owners act as if it's their own business and will do what it takes to make it successful.

THE RITZ-CARLTON

Too much turnover is expensive. Ritz-Carlton has estimated it costs $4,200 to hire and train a new employee, and their efforts to create and maintain engagement as a company have paid off. In the hotel industry, average turnover is a staggering 65 per cent; at Ritz-Carlton, it's 24 per cent. They aren't paying crazy-high wages or bribing people. Their credo says it all: *ladies and gentlemen serving ladies and gentlemen.* They treat their employees like they matter. People stay for the right reasons.

Back to my early career worries about how long I stayed at a company. Research shows that a sweet spot exists for employees: too short and the company loses money on the employee; too long and there is a decrease in engagement.

There are studies that show engagement tends to drop with one's length of service. It's possible that they are getting less development opportunities, seeking less development, and/or are not listened to as much. We'll talk about these factors; it may be possible to avoid this drop-off of engagement with very long-term employees.

What Engagement Looks Like in Successful Companies

Zappos is the successful shoe retailer that was acquired by Amazon in 2009 but remained a

wholly owned subsidiary under the very capable hands of CEO and founder Tony Hsieh. Zappos has created a whole culture of engagement to the point that they run workshops for outsiders wanting to hear more about their "secret sauce." The magic is that they really believe how important it is to treat employees right and, having taken their company tour several times, I can tell you that you can definitely feel it when you are there.

Well-run companies like Zappos are proud of what they are doing with their culture. Even the people running the tours are engaged and transparent about what makes Zappos a great place to work.

MARS Mars, Incorporated, the largest privately owned business in the world, understands the best way to create engagement:

- Start at the top: senior leaders have to commit to focusing on people.

- Choose the right champions for engagement: select a network of associates across the company who are engaged, passionate, and make things happen.

- Set a bold vision for engagement to be a business initiative, not just a numerical target.

- Energize and involve HR as consultants to leaders and managers.

Mars, Incorporated, one of my longest-term clients, is a company I admire for their innovative thinking. They shaped a great deal of my understanding of engagement and the processes I've developed. Early on, we talked about the need to turn to the associates who were giving feedback and allow them to have an active role in identifying actions that would make a difference. Then it's critical that the company follow up on these actions.

| *"You are what you do, not what you say you'll do."* CARL JUNG

In other words, listen to people and then *do something*. It's really not much more complicated than that.

At Mars, the commitment is real. I worked with a group at Mars who was doing the seemingly small task of creating a robust intranet. They made even this job into a chance for engagement. It was so much a part of their culture that they naturally went about asking their stakeholders what they wanted, gathering feedback, talking to people about what success would look like, and being open to input and feedback. Most importantly, the group gathered concerns early, made sure they had all the information, and were willing to make changes. I was reflecting that this is what real engagement looks like.

This begins to give you a feel for what that nebulous word "engagement" looks and feels and sounds like when it exists. Often, the soft stuff like engagement or people skills are hard to measure. We struggle with the idea that everything should be quantified, and we want to be able to efficiently look at engagement and measure change. However, as we develop an understanding of how to assess engagement in organizations through conversation and listening, we'll see that the soft stuff may be hard to measure, but it is really hard to miss once you are looking for it.

4

The Challenge of Measuring the Soft Stuff

Employee Experience and Engagement Are Hard to Measure

Aside from measuring loose direct benefits of employee engagement, like lower turnover, less time lost to accidents, and less shrinkage (theft), most of the benefits are challenging to actually measure. Employee engagement is not measurable like technical numbers: total sales, profits, and losses. Experience is not a quantifiable thing. It would be like going to see an amazing movie in which you cried, laughed, sat on the edge of your seat, and forgot what time it was or what day it was while you were watching—and then when you walked out of the theater someone asked you to rate the comfort of the seats from 1–10. They will get a number but not a measure of your experience.

In the world of measuring engagement, surveys can measure many things. These engagement surveys are typically given once a year, and then the numbers are assessed. In some companies, you

"The soft stuff is the hard stuff!"

GABOR NAGY, PHD

may not even know you were doing an engagement survey because they don't always look like one. At Amazon, employees are peppered with an engagement question every day to take mini-pulses of how things are going. Zappos does a monthly engagement survey. Some companies create custom surveys hoping that coming up with their own questions will make for a more relevant result.

Even administered in different ways, surveys are not the best way to improve the employee experience. There are some basic issues with the whole survey process. You're not getting into the nuances of how the survey taker interprets the question, their mood, or what is going on in their life. It's also very difficult to create questions that measure what you think you are measuring, especially across languages and cultures. These are issues not just with engagement surveys, but with any kind of self-report studies. People are notoriously unreliable when they think they can game the assessment tool and tell you what they think you want to hear.

I don't mean this to be depressing. I'm telling you how hard engagement is to measure with statistics and surveys specifically because there is a better way, and I want you to understand why.

When you are with people, alone or in groups, having a discussion, you can see and hear things that a survey cannot assess. You can see that someone has dark circles under her eyes and you can ask why. You notice that someone else looks distracted and you can ask about it. You're able to set context for people's responses. You can react to their answers and ask follow-up questions and find out more than you ever thought possible. People love to be heard, and very few people feel heard when filling out a questionnaire.

The Power of Conversation

Measuring soft stuff, such as how engaged people are and what their experience is, requires a focus on people. A *real* focus on people, through conversations. So, if you want to measure the impact of what you're doing, how you're doing, then ask the employees, not the managers. There is a temptation to skim the top of the organization and leave the masses of people alone. Sometimes leaders speak to their direct reports or managers because they are unsure of what or how to ask, or what they'll do when they hear things that aren't good.

What do you ask them? Try these questions:

- How are things going?
- What's working?
- What's frustrating or getting in the way?

There are some people, myself included, who would suggest hearing the stories directly is much more powerful and impactful than the hard data anyway.

We've become less and less comfortable with talking to each other and more and more distant in our work cultures. Surveys don't mitigate that trend. The only way we get to real, positive culture change is when we learn to speak to each other and listen to each other. Gallup recently published an article on their website with the title "Do Your Measures Make Employees Mad? Or Motivate Them?" I think they get it.

I worked in one factory as a consultant and the employees expressed the complaint that their manager walks throughout the factory, and is visible, but doesn't know anyone's names. Another manager would walk through and say, "Hey Manny, how's your son's soccer season?" The difference that simple gesture of human connection made was huge. It's an important step to know the people as people, and not as just employee 1367 who works in packaging. This is so elementary and easy to fix, but you would have to know the story, the context, the *why* of their upset to fix it.

If this makes you nervous, you're not alone. People are scared to talk to each other for reasons that range from being an introvert, to being afraid they will be asked something they don't know the answer to, to being afraid that they will mess it up, to a belief that people won't want to talk to them. Like lots of things, like fear of public speaking, it gets easier with practice. You do get over being nervous and you get better at being curious, asking questions, and listening and discussing. And you actually begin to enjoy it.

Structuring these conversations can make the conversation easier if it's uncomfortable or there is a lack of trust between managers and employees. This is a good part of what I do when I work with clients on engagement. Start with a structured conversation around how it's going, how things have changed, maybe using the last survey as a milestone, then ask how it could be better and make micro changes (Google calls these "experiments" so it doesn't feel so daunting) and do check-ins. Once trust is established, these conversations can be more casual.

5

Understanding
the Basics of
Design Thinking

D ESIGN THINKING IS an important concept to understand
because it directly relates to empathetically listening to people
and seeing things from their point of view. For example, if you
have worked somewhere for a long time, how can you possibly know
or remember what the experience is like for the newly hired unless
you talk to them?

Design thinking is not rooted in design in terms of aesthetics,
but rather based on a deep understanding of the principles of empathy, simplicity, and iteration as a means of problem-solving. Design
thinking is about creating solutions that deliver maximum value to
the customer; in the case of employee experience, this means focusing on the employee as the customer.

Creating new solutions to enduring problems can be difficult.
Design thinking gives us the tools and processes we need to focus
our efforts where they will add the most value, helping us arrive
at better solutions and discover questions that will more effectively
address business objectives and customer needs.

"Design thinking is a human-centered approach to innovation that draws from the designer's toolkit to integrate the needs of people, the possibilities of technology, and the requirements for business success."

TIM BROWN, CEO OF IDEO AND AUTHOR OF *CHANGE BY DESIGN*

Design Thinking Components

Design thinking is perhaps best understood as a means of 1. effectively identifying a problem; and 2. arriving at a solution that lives in the intersection of three unique factors.

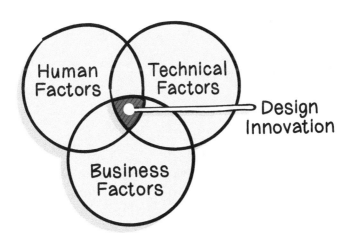

Human Factors

Rooted in empathy, human factors are the most frequently overlooked component of problem-solving in business. The human factors of a problem are the often unexpressed, unidentified, or ignored components rooted in human experience.

These are the attitudes, behaviors, values, and frustrations that often cannot be captured by point-blank questions, but instead must be carefully and thoughtfully excavated and observed. These can be viewed as guiding principles and inspiration.

Technical Factors

Technical factors can be understood by what is technologically and financially feasible—the solutions within reach for a business at a given point in time. These can be viewed as constraints.

Business Factors

The strategic components of a given solution—where a solution that will meet a consumer's need will also fulfill business goals and drive strategic outcomes.

Design thinking is rooted in the exploration of each of these components; where business factors may be a given, human factors require discovery and technical factors are often only discovered through ideation, iteration, and testing.

Phases of Design Thinking

Design thinking includes a framework for how to approach problems, beginning with accurately defining what you want to solve, and ending with a viable solution. While all of these steps may not be applicable to every project, the process is a useful foundation for approaching any challenge.

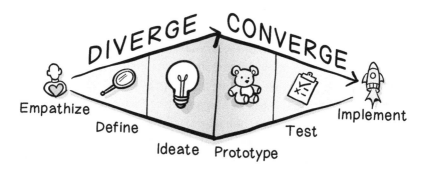

The model has six phases and nicely ties in with another model I use frequently, which is based on Sam Kaner's work in participatory decision-making. We will talk more about this model in Chapter 22, but the idea is that in the initial phases of both decision-making and design thinking, the goal is to create as many ideas as possible. You may know this concept from brainstorming: no idea is a bad idea! And then, when you start to think about how you will test these ideas, you need to narrow down or converge these ideas into the ones that have the most merit.

Before You Start, Define the Scope

When you begin to use design thinking, it is important to understand the constraints, background, and complexities of a given subject or problem. Sometimes this is known as scoping.

To begin scoping, you may want to consult experts, conduct research, or interview your clients. You're looking to expand your perspective to discover what has been considered before and what you do not currently know, as well as to identify the components of a given problem or subject.

Depending on the subject and your own background, you may also want to identify what your own biases or assumptions may be, so that you can be proactive in identifying their interference.

PHASE 1. Empathize; or, "a fish doesn't know it's wet"

Building empathy is at the root of observation. It can involve many components, including many types of interviewing, data analysis, and, yes, simple observation. This must be done with the utmost care so as to avoid solution laddering, and it can be used to uncover hidden needs, frustrations, or behaviors.

Oftentimes, what is not said can be just as powerful and meaningful as what is said, as the most important behaviors may not be recognized with the users themselves. This can also be uncovered through observation—what can you observe about a person, event, or place that would otherwise go unnoticed? What do they spend their time or attention on? What do they seem to ignore?

Likewise, data can be used to identify trends that may be missed by users. However, the goal of this step is to cultivate an understanding of the human need behind a problem.

PHASE 2. Define; or, "ask a better question"

Step back from what you've learned and redefine the problem. Often, we are given a problem or goal as a starting place, but here we redefine the objective in order to meet a human need.

For example, "We need to design a better web portal" may be reframed as "How might we design a tool that better informs our customers about the resources available to them?" The best questions ask, "How might we...?" and are rooted in a human need, rather than a business objective.

PHASE 3. Ideate; or, "there's no such thing as a bad idea"

Now that you've thoroughly identified the box in which you're working, you have the opportunity to step outside of it to identify potential solutions. There are many tools for doing so, but the most important principles of design thinking are to start with what draws your curiosity, think big first (you can always get smaller), explore solutions through play, and withhold judgment. After that, the team can discuss and agree upon the "best" ideas to test in the following phase.

PHASE 4. Visualize; or, "build a model"

Here we work to make something, anything, real. Ideally, multiple things. The goal of this phase is to understand which components of your ideas work and which don't. In this phase, you begin to weigh the impact versus feasibility of your ideas through feedback on your prototypes.

PHASE 5. Test; or, "test it and see if it floats"

Then we can validate our ideas within the team itself, with stakeholders, or even with unbiased outsiders. The aim of this phase is to identify the best possible solution that addresses the various pain points and needs that emerged in the previous phases.

PHASE 6. Implement; or, "try it out"

These solutions can be either accepted, improved, re-examined, or rejected on the basis of users' experiences. This phase also allows the team to better understand the inherent restraints of a given project, and to develop a better/more informed perspective on how real users would behave, think, and feel when interacting with a solution.

This phase is the longest, and will repeat itself innumerable times before arriving at what appears to be the best solution that will meet the human, business, and technological considerations within a project.

As we move into talking more about culture in the next section, it's important to leave our discussion of measuring engagement by reiterating that you really can assess engagement. Maybe not through surveys, but you can. You assess engagement conversationally. It makes sense that you understand engagement by understanding the culture in which it exists, more like an investigative journalist than a statistician. You would never want to read a movie review that told you just the statistics about a movie—how much it cost to make, how much it made in the first week of release, how much each star was paid, and how long it was—because how would it help you to decide whether or not to go? But if someone tells you it is a love story and you will feel wonderful when you leave, then you go buy tickets. The same is true of engagement and the culture in which it occurs. You want to know how you will feel, and conversation tells you that.

The Employee Experience Lifecycle

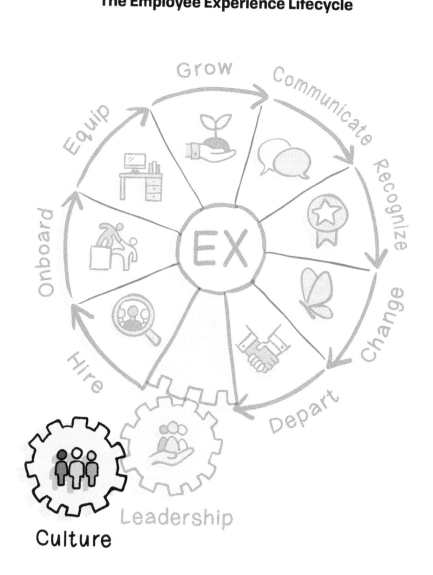

2

Culture

6

What Do You Mean by Culture?

HAVE PROBABLY REPEATED Peter Drucker's quote over 1,000 times. Without a strong culture, the rest of what leaders focus on in terms of results, mission, and business strategy won't matter a bit. And, if I get no other memorable point across in this chapter, remember this: the CEO establishes the culture and can champion changes that result in culture changes. Leaders from the CEO down are responsible for reinforcing this culture throughout the organization.

The average person thinks about culture in terms of a geography one may descend from, like the German culture or Thai culture. Organizational culture is similar in some ways and different in others. In organizations, this thing called culture seems to be getting much more focus recently; yet people still describe it in very vague terms, like "how things are done around here" or "the organization's personality." The term "culture" is even being integrated into job titles, like "Director of Culture Transformation" or "Chief Happiness Officer" at Zappos (we'll look more at one of my favorite examples in a bit).

"Culture eats strategy for breakfast."

PETER DRUCKER, MANAGEMENT CONSULTANT

Culture is the soup in which employee experience swims. If you want people who work for and with you to love their work, then you need to really know and understand your culture. It impacts every moment of your employees' lives. I've heard it said that if you're part of an organization, trying to describe the culture is like asking a fish to describe water: it's very difficult. And to extend the metaphor—fish don't necessarily notice the water, unless it is dank and gross. And by then they are probably not doing well. Learning to notice and pay attention to culture is a crucial leadership skill.

> *"Corporate culture matters. How management chooses to treat its people impacts everything—for better or worse."* SIMON SINEK

One of the most referenced models about organizational culture was created by management consultant Edgar Schein. Culture sits above the waterline, and what really happens sits below the surface.

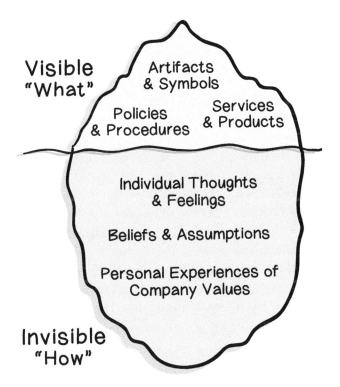

Visible "What"

Artifacts & Symbols

Policies & Procedures

Services & Products

Individual Thoughts & Feelings

Beliefs & Assumptions

Personal Experiences of Company Values

Invisible "How"

The visible things above the water line include physical and known items like artifacts and symbols, policies and procedures, services and products. These can be considered the espoused values or the "what" of an organization: vision, mission, strategic plan, organization chart, business plan, and operating policies. It's what you actually see when you walk into a company—how people are dressed, how the office space is configured, what's on the walls.

Underneath the surface is what actually happens, how things actually work. These are the unspoken and taken-for-granted things in your organization. It's how each of us makes sense of what we think is expected of us, and so subconsciously that we may not even have words to describe it. These are the "how" of the organization: how people think, feel, their beliefs, assumptions, and values that all incorporate the history of the organization.

Each of us experiences culture when we walk into a workplace, whether it's our own or another business or company. Pay attention the next time you walk into any business: what's the *feeling* you get when you walk in the door, from what you see and hear?

 I've taken a few tours of the Zappos headquarters and when you enter the building, one of the things you notice is that they have the bottoms of neckties cut off with people's names on them tacked on a wall. It's part of their culture that if you come to work in a necktie, they cut it off, in a way that is supposed to be casual and lighthearted. Then, once you get past the ties, they walk you through their workplace and they're open to you being there and taking pictures. This is unusual, as I have had to have an employee walk me to the bathroom at other companies so that I would not steal their intellectual property with my phone camera.

At Zappos, the senior leaders are right there, working with the other people. There's an area called Monkey Row where all the C-suite folks are. But it's open seating, too. These things may seem small, but those are all part of culture, as you can see from the iceberg chart above.

You can feel it, also, when you go into a place that is not as playful as Zappos. I visited John Deere headquarters in Moline, Illinois. The building is mid-century architecture, very cool, and on the walls there's all this incredible art. You immediately have some knowledge about the culture. They may be more formal than Zappos, but their building and their set-up also give some insight into their culture.

The Container Store posts their values on the wall near the register, and when you read them, you can see how their employees demonstrate their "employees first" culture. It is demonstrated by how thoughtfully they treat their customers.

You hear the term "culture" referred to all the time—"they have a culture of fear" or "we have a data-driven culture." The point is, there's never *not* a culture. It can be healthy or unhealthy, but it's there and everyone knows it, even if they're not yet able to articulate it. Either way, it's impacting leaders, customers, employees, suppliers, and anyone else who comes into contact with the organization. It's up to you to become aware of it and its impact.

Is your culture helping to achieve your goals? Is it causing unintended consequences? You can have the best strategy in the world, but if your culture does not support it, forget it. You won't get where you want to go.

The best way to understand an organization's culture is to go in with the mindset of a cultural anthropologist. You sift through all the inputs, both above and below the water line from the iceberg model, and you begin to feel what is there. Some things are just noise, but most of what you will find are signals that add up to a culture. Some of what you can look for or listen for are below.

> *"The only thing of real importance that leaders do is to create and manage culture. If you do not manage culture, it manages you, and you may not even be aware of the extent to which this is happening."*
> EDGAR H. SCHEIN, CONSULTANT AND AUTHOR OF *HUMBLE INQUIRY*

Here are some important things to know about culture:

- The culture is owned by the CEO. Period.
- The culture must be anchored to a compelling purpose.
- The culture should be intentional and values-based—what's the story we want people to tell about what it's like to work here?
- Culture is acted out via behaviors; it's hierarchical, meaning the top leaders set the tone—by what they do—for what is expected.
- I'm a big fan of storytelling and the power it has to help convey a concept. Culture is one of those concepts where real examples can help. Here are a few of my favorite culture stories.

Examples of Cultures That Work

 I'm a longtime fan of Zappos. For those who don't know about this amazing company, here's some background. Zappos started in 1999 as an online shoe company based in downtown Las Vegas. Most of their workforce is either on the phone or on a computer, fulfilling orders. CEO Tony Hsieh has been globally recognized for their focus on culture, engagement, and happiness, which he described in detail in his book *Delivering Happiness* and which he speaks about regularly. Zappos was so successful, it was acquired by Amazon in 2009 and left as a wholly owned subsidiary (in other words, don't mess with what's working).

Zappos's culture is built on transparency. Here are some of the things that struck me when I took their public tours:

- Each of the office spaces is personalized to the employee (including a spirit pole), the only rule being "don't offend others." You will see small license plates that say "Zappos" and "registration stickers" for each year they have worked there.

- There's onsite tech support (think Apple Genius Bar) for employees to get help with their work computers.

- They have a service desk called "HelperZ," which helps with such things as employee dry cleaning and acquiring Vegas show tickets.

- They have designed their office so there's only one entrance, so employees see each other and can have "serendipitous moments" with one another.

- There's a hallway called "Recognition Alley," where t-shirts are displayed for each year with a different design done by an employee.

- They have set up a charity library, where business book titles (in multiples) are selected by Tony and Fred (Tony's colleague) and sold to employees and guests for $10 each.

- Each month all the book proceeds go to a selected charity.

- A subsidized bistro is available and serves breakfast, lunch, and dinner.

- There's a space called "skypark," which has Astroturf grass, hammocks, and games for employees to unwind and relax.

- An onsite Goals Coach, who has the only office with a door, is available to all employees to help with professional and personal goals (which can range from learning a new role to losing weight)—access is provided for 30 days, 30 minutes once a week.

- The Customer Loyalty Team members (CLTs) don't have scripts or call time requirements—they are given the freedom to take as long as they need to meet the needs of the customer and empowered to help with anything. They have personal emotional connection (PEC) incentives for customers—things like postcards, cookies, and flowers that the Zappos Supplies Team takes care of sending out. In other words, these CLTs are very clear on what "bad service" looks like.

One of my very favorite things Zappos does is an annual Culture Book. This tradition started a few years after they began, and each year employees are asked to describe, in a few paragraphs, what the Zappos culture means to them. They are asked to indicate if they want their answers to be anonymous, and are requested not to discuss their responses with each other. The question prompts are:

- What is the Zappos culture?
- What's different compared to other company cultures?
- What do you like about our culture?

Now, this could sound like an engagement survey, but here's where it completely differs.

These responses are compiled into a book, which looks almost like a high school yearbook. Along with the responses, the book is filled with photographs of employees and events within the company and the community over the previous year. Many companies, if they even produced such a book, would keep it within the company. But Zappos gives this book out widely to prospective employees, vendors, customers, and visitors for free. In other words, Zappos is proud of their culture and want to promote it; they know stories are the best ways to teach people about their very intentional culture.

"Your culture is your brand and your character." TONY HSIEH, CEO, ZAPPOS

 Google makes employees feel special the minute they are hired by giving them a special name—they are known as "Googlers." In fact, new employees are technically called "Nooglers." As Laszlo Bock, former SVP of People Operations, describes in his book, *Work Rules!*, there are three core factors that make up Google's culture:

1. Mission: At Google, people connect with the aspirational mission that drives the organization and the Googler's behavior. Googlers are asked to discuss what the mission means to them personally.

2. Transparency: A core philosophy of Google since the beginning is "people are good"; therefore, if you hire smart people, you should be sharing more information than you may be comfortable with, including celebrating failures so it becomes okay to talk about them and learn from them. Sharing the goals of the company allows people to understand how what they do matters.

3. Voice: It's important at Google to create ways for people to not only get information, but also to ask questions and express their views. Since the very beginning, Google senior leaders, Sergey Brin and Larry Page, have held weekly all-hands meetings where they share cool things that are happening within Google, and any employee can ask questions directly of the executives.

NETFLIX There's a famous, almost mythical culture slide deck, "Netflix Culture," that is circulated by CEO Reed Hastings, in which he details how he hires, fires, and rewards employees. "It was written so that employees could have clarity about what's important for success, what to expect from each other, and to honestly tell the truth about how the company really operates," says Patty McCord, Netflix's former Chief of Talent, who helped create the deck. They made the deck public on SlideShare in 2009, with continual updates.

Netflix uses the deck as a recruiting tool. Every job candidate is required to read the Netflix Culture deck. Netflix shared it widely to allow honest conversations with potential candidates about what matters to the company. It's a more honest way to start a relationship, as people are looking for company culture and leadership.

What is interesting about all three of these examples is how transparent and clear each company is about their culture. You can go online and find most of this information, if not more. They are all very clear about the culture they believe in—being clear is key to having a strong, intentional culture.

"Your last 100 hires is your culture." RON STORN, VP-PEOPLE, LYFT

When Culture Isn't Working

Culture can go wrong, of course. There can be organizational crisis if the culture is no longer intentional, or if there's a disconnect between what the organization says it believes it values and what it actually does. Remember Enron? This was their list of organizational values:

- Respect
- Integrity
- Communication
- Excellence

And everyone knows how that turned out. There's a big difference between the intent of these values and the impact of how they were interpreted and executed. Apparently "integrity" meant something different to Enron employees than most of us think of when we use that word.

Signs your culture isn't healthy:

- Employees fear taking risks and/or fear getting fired.
- Employees only give positive feedback and get defensive when given suggestions for improvement.
- People feel used rather than valued.
- Talented people only put in average effort.
- Employees form cliques, blame others, and are overly competitive with each other.
- Communication lacks; bad news is shared too late.
- There's a lack of authenticity and honesty.

There's also the challenge of having a subculture of the organization in conflict with the overall culture. For example, the occupational subculture of engineers can be quite different than the company; this conflict comes into play in important areas like safety versus productivity.

Here are five big trends that drive culture today:

1. Learning culture.
2. Sense of purpose.

3. Being inclusive and diverse in every way (heritage, gender, age, thinking styles).
4. Regular feedback.
5. Servant leadership, being purposeful and collaborative.

In other words, you can't have a sustainable organization that values results, outcomes, and numbers more than people. It will catch up with you. This kind of bumbling culture happened a lot when the market was down—in 2008 and right after. The culture was dog-eat-dog and people only stayed in jobs because they had to, but the minute the market rebounded people went to look for other jobs.

I know of a tech company that had layoffs every quarter right before the quarterly reports so that they could report higher earnings. It may have looked good to shareholders, but it turned people against the company and created an environment where people were always fearful for their jobs. And so work was not done as well, there was little innovation, and they needed to keep doing things that looked good on paper but hurt people, thereby creating a downward spiral of culture.

If you want to have a healthy company, you need to pay attention to the long game. You need to take care of your people, your community, and the world. A lot of the metrics we need, like bottom line and shareholder value, will come if you take care of the people. Then they will innovate. They will be engaged.

Creating Cultures of Excellence

How can you create a culture of excellence? Walt Disney World General Manager Marylouise Fitzgibbon, formerly GM of the W Hotel in Fort Lauderdale, describes how to create a culture of excellence:

- Have a strong *Vision*.
- *Listen* before you talk—learn to listen.
- *Over*-communicate.
- *Learn* constantly.
- Give *Feedback*—constantly and consistently.

- Set clear *Expectations.*
- Anchor your culture to the organization's *Purpose.*

So, who is ultimately responsible for setting the tone for culture? Right, the CEO.

Outlined in the following chapters are the key elements that make up the culture. Here are a few examples of all these pieces put together...

 **Purpose**—Connect people to what's important in their lives through friendly, reliable, and low-cost air travel.

Vision—To become the world's most loved, most flown, and most profitable airline.

Values

LIVE THE SOUTHWEST WAY
- Warrior spirit
- Servant's heart
- Fun-LUVing Attitude

WORK THE SOUTHWEST WAY
- Safety and reliability
- Friendly customer service
- Low costs

 **Purpose**—We strive to offer our customers the lowest possible prices, the best available selection, and the utmost convenience.

Vision—To be Earth's most customer-centric company, where customers can find and discover anything they might want to buy online.

Values

- **Customer Obsession:** We start with the customer and work backwards.

- **Innovation:** If you don't listen to your customers, you will fail. But if you only listen to your customers, you will also fail.

- **Bias for Action:** We live in a time of unheralded revolution and insurmountable opportunity—provided we make every minute count.

- **Ownership:** Ownership matters when you're building a great company. Owners think long-term, plead passionately for their projects and ideas, and are empowered to respectfully challenge decisions.

- **High Hiring Bar:** When making a hiring decision, we ask ourselves: "Will I admire this person? Will I learn from this person? Is this person a superstar?"

- **Frugality:** We spend money on things that really matter and believe that frugality breeds resourcefulness, self-sufficiency, and invention.

Culture pays off. While it might take a little work to dig into what it is, it's worth it. If you don't manage culture, it will manage you. It may have a longer payoff, but stick with it. Culture is also malleable. All the places you notice it are the places you could change it. If culture is a feeling, then what else do we need to know about it? What can people do to imagine a better culture than the one that exists now? We will explore that as we continue talking about culture, starting with what it means to have a vision.

7

An Audacious Vision

What We Mean by Mission, Purpose, and Vision

The majority of my consulting life has been helping teams and organizations clarify their vision and the strategies they will use to get there. I'm repeatedly astounded by two things. The first is how many people don't understand the distinction between the organization's mission, purpose, and vision, often using the terms interchangeably. The second is the amount of energy spent on finding the perfect words to describe the vision, overcomplicating it. Comparatively, there is a lack of thinking on how to communicate and engage the people who do the majority of the work to achieve the vision.

Here are the best definitions I know so that we can all be on the same page. Later I will give some examples of each.

Mission is the reason your organization exists. It is not a moveable thing, but instead focused and foundational. Mission is internally focused—what would go away from the planet if we stop doing this thing we are here to do?

"Passion fuels the rocket; vision directs the rocket to its ultimate destination."

CARMINE GALLO, *FORBES*

Purpose is understanding the "why" of the company in a deep sense: why we're here, why we do what we do, and what difference we hope to make for others as a result of doing what we do. It is outward-focused—it has nothing to do with shareholder value or the bottom line.

Vision is an aspirational goal of where we want to get to. If you put them on a straight line, Mission would be point A, Vision point B, and in between would be a rubber band, pulling them together. That rubber band is strategy.

Employees must trust that someone—their leaders—know where they're going. They need to understand the mission and the vision of the organization from the people who lead them. From this, employees can know how what they do connects to the bigger picture of the organization. The power of knowing the bigger picture can be summarized in a classic story about the power of vision I heard years ago.

The Cathedral Story

A man came upon a construction site where three people were working. He asked the first, "What are you doing?" and the man replied, "I am laying bricks." He asked the second, "What are you doing?" and the man replied, "I am building a wall." As he approached the third, he heard him humming a tune as he worked and asked, "What are you doing?" The man stood, looked up at the sky, and smiled. "I am building a cathedral!"

With my clients, I assume they have a mission, a reason they exist and do the work they do. So I try to stay out of the swamp of mission—because without it, they wouldn't hire me. However, I work hard to help clarify the organization's vision because that's where they need to focus to get the people who work there engaged and energized, like the man who knew he was building a cathedral.

Organizations need to continuously refresh their vision—to understand if they are shooting for the moon, where exactly the moon is right now. Let's say the mission is the sun. It's stable, it lights the way, it's the center of gravity for the organization's solar system. The vision is the moon. It keeps moving, it controls the tides, it has a progress and a pattern and you need to understand where it will be to shoot for it.

NETFLIX Let's think about a company like Netflix. Their mission is to be the world's leading internet subscription service for enjoying movies and TV programs. They started out providing DVDs in the mail, which was revolutionary at the time. And then things changed. Streaming content came around and no one wanted or needed to wait for a DVD to show up in the mail. Netflix needed to change their vision and strategies in order to move with the times. Clearly they did or they would have gone the way of Blockbuster, another service with a similar mission that didn't see the writing on the wall of streaming content and lost their market share because of it.

What did Netflix pay attention to that worked? The factors that go into understanding your vision and keeping it current are simple. What external pressures—government, economic, customer driven, technology, and other trends—impact your work? What are the internal factors such as the changing demands of employees, internal technology, and how you do business? An organization with a good grasp of vision will be responding to the market pressures and adjusting their vision to reach for the moon, because they know where the moon is.

None of this is about finding the perfect seven or eight words that encapsulate what you know. It's about a feeling. Do you know enough to create a feeling of what it will be like in the future? Like Netflix, you need to be able to say, it feels like this: getting content to people to enjoy in the way they want it. If you are spending your time wordsmithing those words rather than moving on to the strategies to achieve it, you may be in trouble.

NETFLIX   **Mission**: The world's leading internet subscription service for enjoying movies and TV programs.

Vision would feel like:
- Becoming the best global entertainment distribution service.
- Licensing entertainment content around the world.
- Creating markets that are accessible to filmmakers.
- Helping content creators around the world find a global audience.

Perspective, Power, Potential

The organization's leadership needs to spend time developing a clear focus on where they want to take the organization. The vision is about the customers and what you're going to do for them.

In order to do this, leaders need to spend some time gaining perspective of what's happened in the past, and what they have learned that will help them to be successful in the future. In my work, from my early training at The Grove Consultants International, we spend time talking through the history going back to a certain point in time: sharing stories of people who joined and left, projects and achievements, even things that were going on in the industry and the world that affected what the business was doing at the time. This is valuable storytelling time, and we don't short-change the time spent because of its value. Graphically capturing this is powerful and helps with organizational learning—this piece often becomes part of onboarding new employees. At the end, we talk about lessons learned in reviewing the history, because often there are patterns that are both helpful and harmful.

There's a lot of power in considering the present—where the organization sits today. The Grove has a template called Context Map that allows teams to think about things all around the organization that are impacting or could impact the business: trends, economic conditions, governmental regulations. I have worked with businesses like Lockheed Martin right before a significant election, when who would be elected would have a great impact on their plans. Understanding the "as is" is just as important as the next step: the "to be."

Finally, the vision of the future is the potential the organization has—having considered both their past and their present, they are able to think about how they would like things to be, what their aspiration is for the future.

Apple

To put a computer in the hands of everyday people.

FedEx

Absolutely, positively, overnight.

IKEA

To create a better everyday life for the many people.

Your Rubber Band Strategy

Robert Fritz, author of *The Path of Least Resistance,* emphasizes how important it is to have a compelling vision that focuses energy on where you want to take the organization rather than what you don't want. Often people say, "We don't want to get eaten by our competitors," or "We don't want to lose market share." These are not visions, and they're dangerous because they don't have any pull to them. Borrowing a concept from Fritz, I often demonstrate this by holding a rubber band and stretching it upward. You want to create enough energy to draw people "upward" rather than a lack of energy that takes you only to the lower end—Fritz would say the universe and our minds won't register the words "don't" or "no." So a vision needs to be positive, generative, and future thinking.

Accompanying any vision must be understandable, doable strategies that are linked to the vision. By "linked" I mean they are totally connected and make sense throughout the organization. Linking the strategies from each team and each department to the organization's strategies is key to achieving the vision. Strategies are the rubber band between mission and vision, and they will pull you into the future.

Objectives/Goals/Strategies/ Measures (OGSM)

Many companies use a business strategy called OGSM (Objectives/ Goals/Strategies/Measures) to create these links. This process is outlined in a book called *The 1 Page Business Strategy*. This simple one-page process has been used at companies such as Procter & Gamble and Mars, Incorporated with excellent results. Using this process, everyone understands how they're contributing to the organization's goals.

OGSM looks like this:
- Objective is a vision (words).
- Goals are measurable (numbers).
- Strategy is how you get there (words).
- Measures are how you know if you go there (numbers).

Cheryl DeSantis, former head of HR at Mars Petcare, says that when you have a direct line of sight throughout the organization to what's important, each person can hold themselves accountable to how they are contributing to the business's long-term goals. The OGSM should be closely aligned with the organization's purpose.

But how is an objective different from a vision? DeSantis explains it this way: "Your vision you want to be longer term, maybe three to five years. But your objective is definitely more focused on the near term." The hardest parts, she says, are making sure you don't take on too many things and creating clear metrics, three to five, to measure against.

Back in 1996, there was a *Harvard Business Review* article called "Building Your Company's Vision" by James C. Collins and Jerry I. Porras. In it, they outlined something called BHAGs, which came from Nike and stood for "big, hairy, audacious goals," things that would make you take a deep breath because it would take some real effort to make these types of goals happen.

BHAGs are a vision of sorts, a bold one. And to get there, you need strategy. I like the process outlined above, the OGSM. It helps you to narrow your vision and your strategy in order to be effective and successful, and it helps you assess those BHAGs and decide if you can take them on.

As humans we want to take on so much stuff at once because we are not naturally good at limiting our options. If we take everything on at once, then we end up failing at everything because we didn't discern what the necessary and sufficient steps were, and we dabbled. We need to limit the strategies we undertake to a number we can do—five is usually the max. And that should be enough to create the tactics or actions you need to get the job done. If you feel like you need one hundred strategies, you may be unclear on your vision and need to go back and re-think it.

Robert I. Sutton, professor at Stanford University (and author of one of my favorite books, *The No Asshole Rule*), says there's great value in simplicity, and there needs to be clarity on what should and shouldn't be done. How many times have you seen more and more strategies and plans made without any discussion of what won't be done? What will you say "no" to? In having these conversations, you understand what the powerful "why" is behind your choices.

"If everything is important, then nothing is important."
ROBERT I. SUTTON, STANFORD PROFESSOR AND AUTHOR OF
THE NO ASSHOLE RULE

Strategies are higher level than tactics or actions. They are your road map. Tactics and actions are your turn-by-turn directions. We have a strategy—drive from California to New York in a week. Tactics are things like, "Oh, let's go see the world's largest ball of string on the way." Or, "Let's go through Cleveland because we want to see the Rock and Roll Hall of Fame."

The plan of tactics and actions needs to be revisited and adjusted even more than the vision. You have to keep checking what is on the road ahead, what the weather is like, what sights are coming up next. You can revise and revise tactics or actions to meet the vision better, and you should. But to do that, there needs to be communication.

"A vision without a plan is just a hallucination. But a vision with a plan will change the world." PROVERB

You Need to Communicate

Communicating vision and strategies is as important as creating them. People need to understand them, feel them, and connect with them. Sharing them allows you to test how bold and specific the vision and goals are, and how concise and consistent you are in communicating them. The bigger the organization, the more thoughtful you need to be in how you will share and get feedback on your plans.

I worked with a large organization that had never written business strategies before. After creating them, we worked hard to create a thoughtful and thorough process for sharing them with the next level of the organization, designed to gather their input and feedback. The process was designed to allow the senior leaders, in teams of two, to have fifteen minutes to give an overview of the strategy—they weren't allowed to use PowerPoint (I will get into how I feel about

PowerPoint later). Once an overview was given to an audience of twenty to twenty-five people, the senior leaders sat at different break-out tables, where the audience discussed the strategies, and gathered feedback, which was captured on table templates, and then summarized on large wall templates. This is a demonstration of everything I think makes good employee experience: clear communication, followed by listening and collaborating.

The process resulted in greater engagement by the next level down, who gave thoughtful input directly to the leaders who had developed the strategies, which they used to refine the strategies further. What this process tells us is that it will always be crucial to talk *and* listen in order to make the vision come alive.

Having a mission and a vision isn't optional. There can't be engagement if employees don't know where they are going. It's impossible to have people see their part in the work you do if they don't understand why you do it and what you are doing to get there. We will talk more in Chapter 18 about how to get the message out, how to have the conversations, and how to hear what people are saying. It may seem that mission, vision, and strategy are not clearly related to engagement, but don't be fooled—you can't have engagement, or a culture that supports it, without them.

8

The Power of Purpose

URPOSE, OFTEN CONFUSED with mission, is at the core of a business—it's the "why" behind the existence of the business. It's what *makes* employee experience. Simon Sinek, in his book *Start with Why* and viral TED talk "How Great Leaders Inspire Action," says, "People don't care what you do, they care why you do it." Inspired organizations, he argues, start from the inside of what he calls "The Golden Circle," getting clear on their "why" before moving out to "what" they do or make.

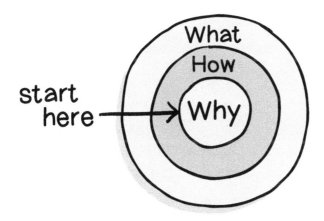

"If you hire people just because they can do a job, they'll work for your money. But if you hire people who believe what you believe, they'll work for you with blood, sweat, and tears."

SIMON SINEK

For example, Sinek says, if Apple communicated like most of us, their message would sound something like this: "We make great computers. They're beautifully designed, simple to use, and user friendly. Want to buy one?"

Instead, according to Sinek, here's what Apple is actually telling us:

In everything we do, we believe in challenging the status quo. We believe in thinking differently. The way we challenge the status quo is by making our products beautifully designed, simple to use, and user friendly. We just happen to make great computers. Want to buy one?

It works, and customers become virulent supporters of the why, seeing themselves as challengers of the status quo, valuers of beauty, and cool computer users. They buy the why.

> *"People don't buy what you do; they buy why you do it."*
> SIMON SINEK, *START WITH WHY*

In other words, it's crucial that you know what your core purpose is first. Here are some questions to consider:

- What do we uniquely enable in the world?
- What does this correct in the world?
- What does this protect in the world?

In the last chapter, we clarified the difference between purpose and vision. For this distinction to make even more sense, you can use the term "core purpose," which gets straight to the point. Sometimes the core purpose gets lost as the company grows or leadership changes. A company's purpose can evolve over time. In a growing company, the purpose broadens; in a shrinking company, the purpose narrows. But it shouldn't change that much, or you're not in the same business.

Here are some great examples of purpose statements—note how they are outward-focused:

Google: To organize the world's information and make it universally accessible and useful.

Wikipedia: A collaborative project to produce a free and complete encyclopedia in every language.

GE: Dedicated to turning imaginative ideas into leading products and services that help solve some of the world's toughest problems.

Life Is Good: To spread the power of optimism.

Patagonia: Build the best product, cause no unnecessary harm, use business to inspire and implement solutions to the environmental crisis.

JetBlue: To inspire humanity—both in the air and on the ground.

Storytelling

During the Second World War, it was assumed that the Germans were close to creating an atom bomb. When President Roosevelt finally launched the Manhattan Project, they recruited the best and brightest young math and science minds from the top universities to provide data for the physicists at Los Alamos. But these students weren't told what they were doing it for. Working long hours with only slide rules and primitive calculators as tools, they were uninspired, inaccurate, and slow. When their leader, Richard Feynman (only twenty-four years old himself), realized they were unmotivated and unclear on the purpose, he conferred with project leader Robert Oppenheimer and they decided to get the highest level of clearance available so they could know the purpose of their important project. Suddenly their work had a very clear purpose: to save the free world. That changed the tone of the project, and they succeeded.

This story demonstrates why having a clear purpose for a team and understanding why we do what we do matters. It also shows the power of knowing what would happen if we didn't exist, and why understanding the higher purpose that connects us to what we're doing matters.

This gets back to the power of storytelling—the ability to tell the compelling reason for doing what you're doing. Studies have shown that charities sending out donation letters, for example, pull two times the donations when the letter is about one person versus using facts and figures about many. This is called the "empathy telescope"— we can put ourselves into the shoes of one person, but can't do it for a huge group. And more and more, people want to believe in the story behind the business, to be inspired by it—to have a clear idea of how your work connects to something meaningful. It becomes personal, in fact.

> *"It's so one-dimensional to have something written down or a poster on the wall. But you bring such texture to the meaning behind a culture through storytelling. And it cannot be just the most senior leaders in the organization."* TAMI MAJER, FORMER MARS ASSOCIATE (NOW WITH DANONE)

Michelle Auerbach, a business storytelling consultant, puts it this way. According to neuroscience, data isn't what calls people to action; story is. Story is what makes our brains pay attention, get on board, and act. No one ever rallied behind a number—facts and figures are too abstract; they don't feel like they can affect you. But if you can get people to feel how the change would feel and see them-selves as heroes in making the change, you will have the power of purpose.

More and more companies are finding that, in order to attract the right talent and create a connection to the company's purpose, every leader (in fact, each employee) benefits from clarifying their own compelling purpose. While this might sound like just too much for you, consider that companies like Google and Unilever have workshops and retreats to help people get a clear sense of their own personal purpose. Seeing that what you care about overlaps with what the company is doing helps individuals feel like they are build-ing a cathedral and not just laying bricks. The driver for the armored truck has to understand the purpose of the organization in a similar way as the CEO and has to understand why they are in business.

 For example, Google's purpose is to organize the world's information and make it uni-versally accessible and useful. One Google employee, Chade-Meng Tan, saw his individual purpose as creating world peace in his lifetime. At first the two might not have seemed to overlap, but both Google and Meng saw the overlap. Google sup-ported Meng in creating the "Search Inside Yourself" program that strove to teach work-based mindfulness to Google employees. It's still the most oversubscribed development program at Google and Meng has gone on to write two books, including *Search Inside Your-self: The Unexpected Path to Achieving Success, Happiness (and World Peace)*. This program works with employees to use mindfulness to improve their own lives, the work they do, and their leadership potential, helping Google to reach its goals with employees who feel their own potential matters. We will talk more about Meng and about how learning and development matters to engagement in future chapters; for now just keep in mind that it can link individual purpose to organizational purpose. Also, know that when there's a disconnect between individual purpose and organizational purpose, people become very unhappy.

The next generation, the one that's coming into buying power, has been researched up and down, back and forth. They're reported to be so curious about the story and the purpose of an organization that they'll change their buying choices based on it. They have so much access to information that they can easily spot inconsistent behavior—so know that you have to have your purpose down and consistently aligned; they want to know you actually walk your talk.

These folks will be the employees of the future, so be aware that the purpose of your organization will only matter more and more over time. And with great purpose comes great engagement. It trickles through the organization, creating meaning in how you do things and meaning out to your customers.

9

Values and Behaviors

BEYOND A COMPANY'S purpose for what it's here to do and a vision of where it wants to get to, there isn't anything more important to employees than how things work day to day. It's their lives we are talking about. Employee experience is where the rubber meets the road when it comes to values and behaviors—these statements and subsequent actions are what really make up the culture of an organization.

The actual company values, and how people treat each other on a day-to-day basis, are demonstrated by who gets rewarded, promoted, or let go in an organization. There must be a clear and direct connection between the nice-sounding values that are posted on the company wall (what we say) and what actually happens. The values of an organization are also present in things like how decisions are made, how people development works, and how meetings are held. They show up through transparent communication; if you are careful, what you say internally should match what you say externally about your company.

The values of an organization convey the true tone of the culture. They're demonstrated by the way leaders communicate with

"We believe that it's really important to come up with core values that you can commit to. And by commit, we mean that you're willing to hire and fire based on them. If you're willing to do that, then you're well on your way to building a company culture that is in line with the brand you want to build."

TONY HSIEH, CEO, ZAPPOS

their managers as well as the entire employee population. The values can also extend to the community outside the organization. Petcare companies like Mars, Incorporated often give back to the local community by advocating for animals. Or take Zappos, which keeps their library of books available for not only employees but also for visitors because they care about learning.

Once internalized, the values become a natural part of employees' everyday language and way of thinking. These operating norms define how employees treat each other. Once you have them, you must commit to live by them.

Johnson & Johnson is a great example of a values-driven organization. They have a credo, which they live and work by. Decisions both small and large are made with the credo, from hiring to budget to learning and development. Anyone who works with them comes across the credo immediately and begins to see how deeply it impacts the organization. J&J does not measure engagement per se, but they do measure how they are doing in adhering to the credo every year, and pay very close attention to the results—supporting the places where the credo score was low, and working to make sure that the entire 140,000 people who work there are living the credo daily. There's a huge copy of the credo right inside the door of the corporate offices that you see as you go in. It lives in every building and in many conversations, and it gives the employees something with which to align their individual purpose.

Consider these great examples of corporate values, all of which are publicly accessible on the internet. By publishing and sharing them, they are inviting people to hold the company to what they say they stand for. They are telling potential candidates *this is what you can expect—are you a good fit with these?* For each of these companies, it's clear the company really thought about:

- What makes us uniquely "us"?
- What do we really believe in, and how do we want our current and future employees to behave to demonstrate these beliefs?

Netflix Values

NETFLIX

Judgment
- You make wise decisions despite ambiguity.
- You identify root causes, and get beyond treating symptoms.
- You think strategically, and can articulate what you are, and are not, trying to do.
- You are good at using data to inform your intuition.
- You make decisions based on the long term, not near term.

Communication
- You are concise and articulate in speech and writing.
- You listen well and seek to understand before reacting.
- You maintain calm poise in stressful situations to draw out the clearest thinking.
- You adapt your communication style to work well with people from around the world who may not share your native language.
- You provide candid, timely feedback to colleagues.

Curiosity
- You learn rapidly and eagerly.
- You contribute effectively outside of your specialty.
- You make connections that others miss.
- You seek to understand our members around the world, and how we entertain them.
- You seek alternate perspectives.

Innovation
- You create new ideas that prove useful.
- You re-conceptualize issues to discover solutions to hard problems.
- You challenge prevailing assumptions, and suggest better approaches.

- You keep us nimble by minimizing complexity and finding time to simplify.
- You thrive on change.

Courage
- You say what you think, when it's in the best interest of Netflix, even if it's uncomfortable.
- You are willing to be critical of the status quo.
- You make tough decisions without agonizing.
- You take smart risks and are open to possible failure.
- You question actions inconsistent with our values.
- You are able to be vulnerable, in search of truth.

Passion
- You inspire others with your thirst for excellence.
- You care intensely about our members and Netflix's success.
- You are tenacious and optimistic.
- You are quietly confident and openly humble.

Selflessness
- You seek what is best for Netflix, rather than what is best for yourself or your group.
- You are open-minded in search of the best ideas.
- You make time to help colleagues.
- You share information openly and proactively.

Inclusion
- You collaborate effectively with people of diverse backgrounds and cultures.
- You nurture and embrace differing perspectives to make better decisions.
- You focus on talent and our values, rather than a person's similarity to yourself.
- You are curious about how our different backgrounds affect us at work, rather than pretending they don't affect us.

- You recognize we all have biases, and work to grow past them.
- You intervene if someone else is being marginalized.

Integrity

- You are known for candor, authenticity, transparency, and being non-political.
- You only say things about fellow employees that you say to their face.
- You admit mistakes freely and openly.
- You treat people with respect independent of their status or disagreement with you.

Impact

- You accomplish amazing amounts of important work.
- You demonstrate consistently strong performance so colleagues can rely upon you.
- You make your colleagues better.
- You focus on results over process.

What I really like about Netflix's values is that they don't just expect the one word to be clear enough to explain what they mean—how many interpretations do you think there are for "integrity"? Netflix uses the bulleted defining statements to explain what their company means by integrity.

Quicken Loans "ISMS"

- Always raising our level of awareness.
- The inches we need are everywhere around us.
- Responding with a sense of urgency is the ante to play.
- Every client. Every time. No exceptions. No excuses.

- Obsessed with finding a better way.
- Ignore the noise.
- It's not about *who* is right; it's about *what* is right.
- We are the "they."
- You have to take the roast out of the oven.
- You'll see it when you believe it.
- We'll figure it out.
- A penny saved is a penny.
- Numbers and money follow; they do not lead.
- We eat our own dog food.
- Simplicity is genius.
- Innovation is rewarded. Execution is worshipped.
- Do the right thing.
- Every second counts.
- Yes before no.

Yes, there's a lot of them. But here is what I love about Quicken Loans' values ("ISMs"): each of them has a further definition of what that one phrase means. They each have a visual icon to remember the ISM. Finally, just the fun way of referring to them as ISMs instead of values shows they have given them some serious thought.

Zappos's Core Values

1. Deliver WOW Through Service.
2. Embrace and Drive Change.
3. Create Fun and a Little Weirdness.
4. Be Adventurous, Creative, and Open-Minded.
5. Pursue Growth and Learning.
6. Build Open and Honest Relationships with Communication.
7. Build a Positive Team and Family Spirit.

8. Do More with Less.
9. Be Passionate and Determined.
10. Be Humble.

Zappos's core values were developed originally as a draft and then shared with employees for feedback. Zappos employees are responsible for holding each other accountable for demonstrating them, and employees are hired and fired according to them. As with Quicken Loans, each value is accompanied by a further description.

The Container Store Foundation Principles

The Container Store

1. I great person = 3 good people.®
2. Communication IS leadership.®
3. Fill the other guy's basket to the brim. Making money then becomes an easy proposition.®
4. The best selection, service & price.®
5. Intuition does not come to an unprepared mind. You need to train before it happens.®
6. Man in the Desert selling.®
7. Air of Excitement.®

If you go into The Container Store, you will find these values framed near the register—the store is proud to share them with the public. That's because the company was structured around these ways to treat their employees, customers, vendors, shareholders, and the community.

Why such a focus on corporate values? I picked companies who lay out what they believe, who mean it, who live by it, and who successfully communicate it to their employees. These values matter because the employees are watching, experiencing, and feeling everything that happens. They are attracted to and proud of the company because of the values. They see an alignment between their personal values and things the organization cares about. That shows up because when you interact with an employee as an outsider you can feel their pride about where they work.

When we talk about how engagement feels, this is the feeling. The employees are clear on the purpose and the values of the place they work. They see what's rewarded, what's valued, how their compensation works, and on what their assessments are based. They hear what's communicated and they feel the connection between what they do and the success of the organization. And you can feel it when you talk to employees with this level of engagement to their values. When you meet with them, or interact with them, they radiate engagement.

There's a truism that leaders don't generally interact with customers. They're dependent on people way down the line, who manage the people who interact with the customers. You need to know that every nook and cranny of an organization feels the values. There's this idea that if you take care of the employees, the employees will take care of the customers. So while it may be true that leaders do not directly meet customers, it is also false that leaders' values don't reach customers. They do, through each and every employee in a company and through the feeling of the company culture.

When we talked at the beginning about how engagement feels and we couldn't define it, this is what we were talking about. Now that you have worked through what engagement is, and what culture is, and how mission, purpose, vision, and values impact the organization, you can better understand what engagement is and how it works.

The Employee Experience Lifecycle

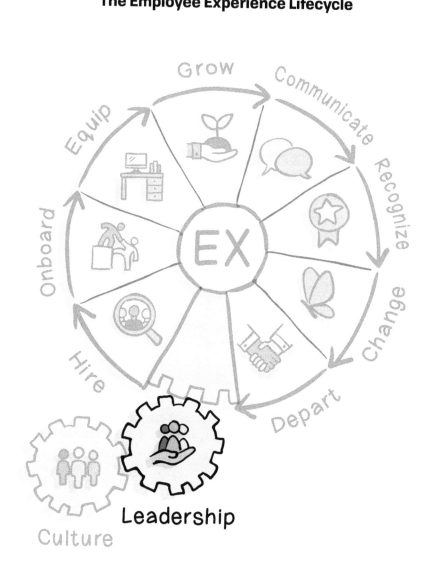

3

Leadership

10

Managers Are Not the Same as Leaders

CRINGE WHEN I hear people confuse and interchangeably use the terms "leader" and "manager." They have very different meanings and very different roles. In the simplest of terms, a manager's role is to focus on the "as is"—to manage the tasks and projects, to fix and improve things. In contrast, a leader's role is to focus on the "to be"—to acknowledge the current reality and declare a new desired reality, to inspire people.

In terms of purpose, vision, and strategies, leaders need to understand and communicate the purpose and vision of their organization, so that managers can make the strategies work. This doesn't always happen smoothly; as consultant Peter Drucker says, "So much of what we call management consists in making it difficult for people to work."

We need both great leaders and great managers in order to have engaged employees, and both need to communicate what they know well to the people who work with and for them. As I used to tell my young daughter (now an adult), "A leader without followers is just bossy." We all know those bossy managers and leaders, and no one wants to be one.

"The key difference between managers and leaders is that managers tell people what to do, while leaders inspire them to do it. Inspiration comes from three things: clarity of one's vision, courage of their conviction, and the ability to effectively communicate both of these things."

JEFF WEINER, CEO, LINKEDIN

Here are lists that summarize the work of leaders and managers so that we can be clear what we are talking about.

Manager	Leader
1. Tells	1. Sells
2. Instructs employees	2. Encourages employees
3. Relies on control	3. Inspires trust
4. Approves	4. Motivates
5. Has objectives	5. Has vision
6. Thinks short-term	6. Thinks long-term
7. Has eye on the bottom line	7. Has eye on the horizon
8. Accepts the status quo	8. Challenges the status quo
9. Establishes rules	9. Breaks rules
10. Minimizes risks	10. Takes risks
11. Focuses on systems and structure	11. Focuses on people
12. Does things right	12. Does the right thing
13. Votes with their head	13. Votes with their heart
14. Sees a problem	14. Sees an opportunity
15. Focused on power and control	15. Focused on influence and inspiration

"Effective leadership is putting first things first. Effective management is discipline, carrying it out." STEPHEN COVEY

Another way to think about the difference can be seen in this graphic, which came out of UCLA professor Iris Firsenberg's talk on leadership. Her point was that if you are successful, you know the *why* behind your work and how to get it done. If you know your

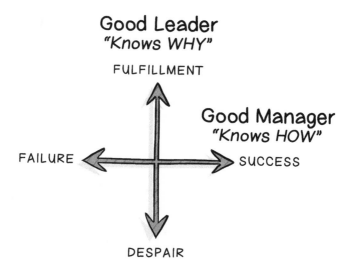

why, then you are a good leader. If you know your *how,* how to do the work, you are a good manager. However, both are necessary. If your organization isn't successfully articulating and communicating both the *why* and the *how,* then you need to figure out how to make that happen.

If you don't know the *how,* you are doomed to failure; if you don't know the *why,* you are doomed to despair. The graphic shows that the way you handle these questions indicates whether you are a good manager or a true leader.

Great Managers

> *"Every employee deserves a great manager."*

The behavior of an employee's direct manager has been proven to have the greatest impact on a team's engagement. In every company

I work with, people say they feel bombarded with more and more things to do, and less time and resources to do them. If the manager can't effectively help control the work that comes to the team as well as take care of the health of the individuals on the team, no one wins.

When you are overwhelmed, your manager isn't giving you priorities that link to the greater *why*. Most companies are great at putting out fires. They are reactionary, and reactionary isn't directed clearly at the *why* of an organization. If you feel pulled in too many directions, it's hard to build a connection between what you do and how to decide what to do and the bigger *why*.

"People join companies but leave managers."

My daughter worked for a volleyball club while she was in college. She is one of those amazing employees—she will always do far beyond anything you expect or ask of her; her need, especially as she gets started in her work life, is to feel appreciated and recognized. When she told me about the boss she had, I was horrified. The boss would exclude her from work opportunities. She would give lucrative assignments to her colleagues and not her. My daughter soon felt disengaged and disheartened; she began doing the bare minimum because there was no point in doing more than that—which is completely against her nature. The company was very lucky—when she decided to leave, she worked hard to find someone to replace her who would match her own standards. Did her manager ever appreciate or recognize her for her efforts? No. This happens frequently, of course: poor managers driving away great employees.

Companies want to bring out more creativity and innovation in their employees. These are the core skillsets for the future that most companies are working to create or nurture in their employees. Creativity and innovation are basically impossible if you have run-of-the-mill disengagement. With even the average kind of "Ho hum why bother?" attitude, it's just not going to be an environment where people are sparked to innovate. What you have is a culture of "Why try? I'm not going to be recognized for it or rewarded for it. I'm not going to see things change or my ideas take off; so, really, what's the point?" Some people will do it anyway, like my daughter—but, mostly, you are just going to shut down people's creativity. They'll check out and stay on your payroll, but you are not getting their full potential.

Let's assume you originally hired smart, creative people. We will talk about hiring for engagement in Chapter 15, but, for now, assume you did it. What's going to motivate them to be creative and engaged throughout their work lives at your company?

Managers and Engagement

 Laszlo Bock, author of *Work Rules!* and formerly in charge of People Operations at Google, describes what he sees as the problem with the manager role in most organizations and what Google did about it. Google is a data-driven company. Everything they do is based on information. They don't believe in "gut feelings" or intuition. So, when I say you can feel what engagement feels like, they would say, nope, let's measure. They also believe that bias can get in the way of good leadership. In fact, Google's philosophy is to remove as much power as they can from the manager, so there's no bias. They try to put employees in charge of just about everything, which Bock describes as "inmates running the asylum," with the goal of not allowing anyone to be able to claim "it's the manager's fault." This ties back to Google's philosophy on hiring the right people. In fact, at Google, the manager cannot make the hiring decision—this is done by committee, whose only incentive is quality in the hiring choice. The outcome is that there is no one above you who is making it hard for you to work, and you have total accountability—which is a lot of freedom and can lead to huge amounts of creativity and engagement.

Even in situations where managers have a lot of power, they can be a force for good. They can share the *why* and the *how* and help their employees see how the work they do lines up with purpose and vision. They can reward employees for engagement, and they can recognize people for what they do right. Employees can be given opportunities to learn from each other. They cross-train, and then they can lead brown bag sessions on topics they know. Managers can invite them into organizing and becoming a leader. And managers can reward it. In other words, they can shape employee experience from the ground up.

My belief is that managers can and should be leaders. Some people say managers are in the middle and stand between leaders and employees, but I don't agree. The workforce of today and tomorrow requires the inspirational skills of leaders, the people and emotional intelligence skills of managers, and the engagement of employees with the greater purpose of the organization. Everybody has to have some leadership skills at whatever level, title or not.

In an organization like I just described, engagement would be high, and productivity, creativity, and innovation are the likely outcomes. I believe this all starts with leadership skills. So, let's see what it is they need to know.

11

Leadership Skills
from the Start

NOW THAT WE'VE established the distinction between managers and leaders, and that everyone needs leadership skills, let's focus on the important role of the leader, starting from the beginning.

 Remember Chade-Meng Tan of Google, who wanted to develop world peace by teaching work-based mindfulness? Well, his purpose really did line up with Google's and he helped to expand an understanding within the company about the components of great leadership. In his program, the very first reason to learn mindfulness at work is to create self-awareness for yourself as a leader and a person. With self-awareness as a leader, anything is possible. The Google program to improve employee experience started a conversation on mindfulness at work that focused on improvement through awareness.

Great leaders are self-aware, taking the time to reflect on how they impact the people around them. Leadership can show up everywhere; it's a skillset and a mindset. You may not want to change your

> ### "Excellence starts with leadership."
>
> **JENNIFER BLACKMON, RITZ-CARLTON**

job in order to change your responsibilities at work, but you may want to up your skill level as a leader. You can lead from any seat in an organization.

Here are some questions I ask leaders about their path, values, and skills. Everyone who has any impact on their co-workers, employees, or customers could benefit from thinking about these questions.

Why do you want to get into leadership?

When I work with leaders, I'll often ask them to share their stories of how they got into leadership. Some people just found themselves drawn to leadership opportunities from a young age, and some were inspired by leaders they had known; others found themselves in these roles because of their own personal values, while others just have a passion for people and are naturally drawn into these positions.

What are your own personal values?

You have to be clear about what you personally believe, what you will always stand for and won't compromise on. We see examples every

day of people who let down their ethical barriers, and others who don't waver. We all want to be and work with the latter. I listened to an interview with a reporter who broke the story on a certain prominent Hollywood executive. She shared that a private investigator tried to get her to waver on her values and the *New York Times'* ethics policies by dangling a lucrative speaking engagement in front of her. Rather than put herself into an uncomfortable position, she responded by saying she was too busy. Had she not been clear on her own values, she could have jeopardized her professional credibility and the important story she later broke.

Early in my career I worked in the public sector, and the guideline we adhered to was "how would it look if what you were doing was on the front page of the newspaper?" Think about the power of that statement, and then think of how many bad things could be prevented if people used this approach to guide their behavior.

Consider your own values and compare them to the organization you work at or would like to work at: are they aligned?

What leaders have you had that you admire, and why?

We are often shaped, willingly or not, by the people we see exhibiting leadership behavior. One of my first managers out of college was a controlling woman who didn't see it as part of her job to guide or mentor me, but instead to belittle me. I vowed never to treat anyone as she treated me. I was fortunate to have had two inspiring managers just a few years later, who encouraged my development, gave me challenging projects, coached me, and trusted my judgment.

I ask leaders to share stories about the leaders they have admired, as often they reflect these qualities in their own leadership behaviors. Their stories are powerful, as they share things they remember about early teachers, sports coaches, and parents, as well as work leaders who inspired them.

How comfortable are you with giving feedback, both positive and negative?

Whether we like it or not, giving feedback is one of the best ways we have to help people grow and develop, as well as course correct. I met a recent college graduate who shared the struggles she'd had as an engineering student working on senior projects—her peers didn't want to give her honest feedback and she didn't want to critique their work either. Yet it's at these times that input is most useful, and when delivered with the intent to improve, it can be invaluable. Ultimately it does no one any favors to let others bumble through mistakes when we see how they can improve.

Now You're a Leader

Most of us learned our leadership skills from the leaders who led us. You have in your head both leaders who have led well and leaders who have led poorly. You are pretty clear on what worked for you and what didn't. If you're aware and give it some thought, you can use this to build your own leadership skills. We'll talk more about this in the next chapter on Conscious Leadership.

You may be a new leader, or thinking about making the leap, or just want to understand what leadership means. Take time to think through and even write out your answers from the questions above so that you start with a clear idea of where you came from and what you believe.

All leaders are going to make mistakes. When you move into a leadership role, you're going to have to be comfortable with not always getting things right. There is a four-stage model that we will talk about more in Chapter 20, but here's what you need to know:

Everyone moves through four stages of learning.

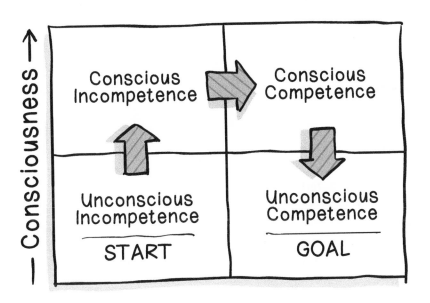

The first stage is unconscious incompetence—you don't even know what you don't know. Then, you realize what you don't know and you become consciously incompetent. Next, you move along, you learn a little more, and you become consciously competent—you have to think about it, but you can do it. Finally, you become unconsciously competent—you can do it without even thinking.

When you first start thinking about your leadership, you will move from unconscious incompetence to conscious incompetence; as uncomfortable as it is to know you're not perfect at what you're doing, it's progress.

You're also dealing with people. That means things are definitely going to go wrong. People are not a PowerPoint deck. You can come back to a deck and it will always be the same. People don't work that way. They're complicated and sometimes challenging. As a leader you'll feel incompetent often, and that's okay. People are difficult and new situations call on new skills. So, whether you're already a leader, a new leader, or thinking about being a leader in the future, there's a lot to learn about engagement, culture, and motivation. As you move into conscious incompetence, I promise practice will take care of the rest.

Early Leadership

> *"With great power comes great responsibility."*

The first leadership position most people generally get is a first-line supervisory role, sometimes called line manager, depending on the industry. This role is unique and critical, as it's the separation of the delegators and the doers. But it carries a lot of responsibility. Consider this list of things first-line supervisors are often responsible for:

- Team building
- Onboarding
- Training
- Quality
- People management
- Planning
- Recognition
- Meetings (planning, running, and attending)

- Communication
- Shifting priorities
- Implementing organizational initiatives

Whatever your title is, if you lead people, you're responsible for getting things done through people. It's no longer you delivering the work yourself; you're doing it through others. You need to inspire them to do their best work when and how you need it. If you can't engage them, you can't be successful.

The biggest mistake leaders make is being afraid to have important conversations: with their employees, their peers, and their own leaders. Leaders generally cite concerns that they won't be able to handle conflict or potential emotional responses, or that they will lose control of the situation. As with most things, these skills can be learned through practice and feedback. And as with most engagement, it comes through conversation—you need to talk to the people who work for you, because just the act of doing so raises engagement.

Servant Leadership

"The first responsibility of a leader is to define reality. The last is to say thank you. In between, the leader is a servant." MAX DE PREE

The gold standard for creating engagement and an experience that employees want to have at work is to be a servant leader. It doesn't matter what you call it, but stripping away the title, you have to work through people and it isn't all about you, the leader. It's not about hoarding power and control, but sharing and being open to ideas. If you get excited that people who work for you move on to higher roles, that they get recognized, that they are rewarded, you are a servant leader.

The term "servant leadership" was coined in 1970 by Robert Greenleaf. The difference from traditional leadership:

TRADITIONAL LEADERS	SERVANT LEADERS
Accumulate and exercise power	Share power
"Top of the pyramid"	"Upside-down pyramid"
People serve the leader	Leader serves the people

When leaders shift their mindset to serve first, they unlock purpose and ingenuity in those around them, resulting in higher performance and engaged, fulfilled employees. By putting the needs of others first and helping them to develop, the servant leader creates an environment where people become healthier, wiser, freer, and more empowered. This is the definition of a culture of engagement.

Nine qualities of a servant leader:

1. Values diverse opinions.
2. Cultivates a culture of trust.
3. Develops other leaders.
4. Helps people with life issues, not just work issues.
5. Encourages people.
6. Sells rather than tells.
7. Thinks in terms of you, not me.
8. Thinks long-term.
9. Acts with humility.

I remember hearing about a company that wouldn't give a new leader a seat in the office until they met a certain number of people within a certain number of days. It was the company's expectation that a leader would focus on meeting people before focusing on tasks. So, the leader had to wander around, getting to know everyone and learning, before settling down to make things happen. This created an environment of engaged leaders and engaged employees. And eventually they got a chair.

It might be obvious, but since leaders create the environment of the organization, servant leaders create engagement.

If you look at those nine qualities in the box above, most are tied to what surveys and research would say create engagement. Listening to people, seeing them as whole people, practicing empathy, supporting people as opposed to directing people—those qualities are part of a culture where people understand how they fit in the organization, feel essential, and want to contribute.

How leaders see people—limited or limitless—is a good arbiter of how they will treat their employees. Servant leaders see people as limitless. They, themselves, are always learning and always growing; they see learning and growing as important in their employees, too. You will later see how these qualities are tied to design thinking and a growth mindset. But how do you become that kind of a leader? How do you make the shift to create the kinds of opportunities that lead to all the goodies you want for your people? You need to be a conscious leader yourself.

12

Conscious Leadership

Crucial Leadership

Knowing all the information you now know about engagement and culture, about what employees experience in their day-to-day work lives, you realize how crucial leadership is. So, how do you want to come across as a leader? The list of traits and skills of a great leader varies from person to person. What is on your list is less important than the fact that you're thinking about it. You need to know how you want to be as a leader, and then put some work into it. It's not going to happen automatically, but that's actually good. If you took the time in the previous chapter to answer the questions about leadership, now is a good time to pull out your answers and see what kind of leader you want to be.

When I do engagement work, and I work with leaders, I push them to start with themselves. They need to consciously reflect on how, as leaders, they will come across to employees. And their awareness increases as they work with me and go through my process.

It all has an impact. And, best of all, it's learnable.

"Be more interested than interesting."

DAVID MELTZER

Leaders model from the top, but no one can do it without support. That's why we work with leaders when we start to talk about engagement with an organization—it just won't happen otherwise. It's one thing to understand what it means to be a leader; it's another thing altogether to do it in a confident and inspirational way. Leaders often fall into the trap of believing that they must have all the answers, while the opposite is actually true. The trick is being willing to ask lots of questions and not know everything. Confidence means you are more curious than critical of those around you. And that leads to incredible engagement.

Empathy is a crucial part of leadership, especially in the practice of conscious or servant leadership. According to Tamara Christensen, a leader in design thinking and the founder of Idea Farm, empathy helps us to focus more on the other humans involved in a situation and less on ourselves.

Christensen says, "If you look at the word *empathy*, and you remove the letters A and H, you're left with *empty*. The thing that most gets in our way when we're trying to listen to other people are our own perceptions, responses, emotions, feelings, ideas, fears about what someone is saying. As leaders we need to empty ourselves of those blockers that take our mind away from being present and listening in the moment: *This is what I think about it. Here's what I'm going to ask about it. Don't they know about this? Have they thought about that? Didn't they hear about this project we did two years ago, et cetera, et cetera, et cetera? Don't they know the impact that has on someone else?* A lot of the obstacles that we experience too deeply, genuinely listening and being in empathy with someone else, have to do with the runaway train of thoughts that's in our head." This "runaway train" experience takes us out of modeling supportive, empathetic leadership and into something that's not so positive for employee experience.

Busy, Busy, Busy

| *"'Busy' has become the new 'fine.'"* JEFF SHINABARGER

These days, I hear the phrase "I'm so busy" coming out of the mouths of everyone, from CEOs to first-line supervisors to new hires. It has become a badge of honor. If you're not busy, then you're doing something wrong, or you have room for more work because you're slacking.

I have made a conscious effort, because I hear this awful phrase way too often, to never ever say it myself. It took me time to consciously realize that when we are not so focused on appearing busy that we can be present and available to support the people with whom we work and bring out the best in everyone.

This is just good leadership. Good leaders free people up to be their best, and they consciously work to model the behaviors they want from their people. So, they say "no." Because if everything is important, then nothing is important.

Leaders need to begin to make distinctions about what's important. Once that's clear, then so is what's not important. I tell clients to find their clear purpose, as we discussed before, and then they can check every priority against their purpose; if it doesn't fit, drop it. The key is to be conscious of what the expectations are for yourself as a leader and for your people and what you have to do to be successful in forwarding the organization's purpose.

> *"Focusing is about saying 'no.'"* STEVE JOBS

Leadership isn't all about doing everything; many people feel like they have no choice but to say "yes" to everything that comes along. But learning to say "no" effectively is a critical skill for a leader to model and to demonstrate to others. Making effective choices is an important tool in managing time and priorities. Sometimes it's easy to feel like you are missing out on something—my dear friend and colleague Janine always refers to FOMO, fear of missing out. As a leader, you need to miss out so other people can shine. You need to help them understand that to do their work well, they are going to miss out on some stuff, too. But all that missing out leaves you calmer and more productive.

Conscious Leadership Attributes

After working with leaders all over the world, I believe there are eight key skills and attributes that conscious leaders need to have:

1. **Authenticity**—being real and genuine with people.

2. **Vulnerability**—not having all the answers, sharing successes and failures.

3. **Transparency**—openness about what's happening and the thinking behind decisions.

4. **Self-Awareness**—being clear on your own purpose and values.

5. **Collaboration**—willingness to work with others and not take all the credit.

6. **Empathy**—the caring, compassion, and empathy that's critical in leading people.

7. **Curiosity**—understanding the need to constantly learn.

8. **Integrity**—doing what you say you will do.

Courageous Leadership

"Courage, the original definition of courage when it first came into the English language—it's from the Latin word cor, *meaning heart— and the original definition was to tell the story of who you are with your whole heart."* BRENÉ BROWN, AUTHOR OF *DARE TO LEAD*

If you've ever watched Brené Brown's TED talks or read her books, you know how inspiring she is. Brené emphasizes how important it is for all of us to demonstrate compassion and empathy—leaders in organizations play a very important role in modeling these qualities. She talks about the danger of pride and the importance of having courage—courageous leadership is having a core set of values and principles that you are not willing to waver on.

I was completely inspired by hearing Mayor Lester Taylor III speak about leadership. Mayor Taylor is the second youngest mayor ever of the city of East Orange, New Jersey. During his campaign, the city's Water Commission Executive Director and Deputy Director were both indicted for falsifying water records. As he began his term, there was tremendous pressure to privatize the commission, but the city's new mayor didn't think this was the right way to go. Acting as a courageous leader for what he felt was right, he removed the entire five-member board from the previous mayor's term and appointed a new board. While there was a lot of pressure to sell the asset, he lobbied to get a $4 million bond to restructure the debt payment over several years and put a $24 million capital investment in the infrastructure. Four years later, the city services not only their own citizens but also neighboring cities at a profit.

I asked Mayor Taylor what lessons he learned from the experience, and here was what he said: "Compassion, humility... sometimes as a leader even if you have the right answer, it's a delicate balance of getting buy-in. You have to be patient with people because everyone likes change until it affects them."

And as for those who had a role in the wrong path, I asked him what he thought. "Government legacies, which are invested in the city, the culture, and have watched past failures—some decisions you make today, you don't know if it's good or bad until months or years from now." In other words, be understanding of the circumstances in which the decisions were made; certainly no one likes to be told they were wrong.

The reason that East Orange was not the second Detroit, falling into a morass of problems and not able to fix them with the current resources, was because Mayor Taylor had the courage to tackle the big issues and make hard decisions. He fired some people because they were not serving the purpose of the city. He took a stand. Mayor Taylor's "no" to the board meant that there was a "yes" for the people of the city. He had an internal moral compass that guided him and that aligned with the city's purpose. He trusted it and aligned to it. Mayor Taylor succeeded because it was about the success of his city. Leaders fail if they believe it's all about them.

Mayor Taylor's Suggestions for Courageous Leadership

- Be *bold*—study the issues and make informed decisions, even if they may not be popular.
- Sometimes the greater good requires tough decisions to be made.
- Recognize that the impact of your decision can be felt for generations to come.
- It's important to do *something*.

"I can accept failure. What I can't accept is not trying."
MICHAEL JORDAN

Building Trust Through Purpose

Most engagement conversations necessitate trust, but many of us are confused about what creates and builds trust. Trust is built or diminished based on a continuous series of conscious and unconscious assessments we make of four leadership qualities that combine to create credibility and build trust:

1. Competence—the experience the leader has.
2. Reliability—does the leader do what they say they will do?
3. Motive—are the leader's interests aligned and transparent?
4. Vulnerability—demonstrating openness to not having all the answers.

When a leader says to the people who work for them, "I trust you," a chemical called oxytocin is released in the listener's brain—as an employee, you can't help but trust back. When trust is demonstrated, for example, when a leader acknowledges their own mistakes, others can't help but return the feeling.

Ask yourself:

- What are you doing to build trust?
- What are you doing that's hurting trust?

Consider this scenario about trust and connection. Douglas E. Morris, in his book *It's a Sprawl World After All*, shares his research on how sprawl is harming America. Back when people lived near where they worked and kids played outside, neighbors got to know each other. But now, with people commuting long distances and kids being shuffled from school to activities all the time, people don't get to know their neighbors. Therefore, they're strangers. And we all remember what Mom told us: "Don't talk to strangers!" But, if we don't talk to them, we don't feel connected to them; therefore, we don't trust them. And it spirals from there.

"I can't work with you if I don't *trust* you, and I can't *trust* you if I don't *know* you."

Your awareness as a leader and your ability to follow the purpose of the organization are what make that experience one of trust and not frustration. Back to Chade-Meng Tan's awareness campaign at Google. Your ability to be self-aware increases your ability to regulate yourself and to respond well to what comes down the pike. You respond in ways that are aware and conscientious, and people begin to see you can be trusted. You build teams through the process of doing real work. For instance, if leadership involves me in the conversation about where we are headed as an organization, and about the strategies to get there, that builds my trust in them. I know my opinion matters and I am involved in crafting the future. Self-awareness leads to the ability to have those conversations, which leads to building trust.

> *"There's no need to be perfect to inspire others. Let people get inspired by how you deal with your imperfections."* ZIAD K. ABDELNOUR, *ECONOMIC WARFARE*

I worked with a client on an engagement process in which people in the organization started out very angry and upset. The process we use helps leaders get very good at listening. We will talk more about that in Part Six, which is about our process. It's important to know that leaders, once they are conscious of their role and how to focus on building trust, can change the entire experience of the people who work for them.

We asked the people, both leaders and employees, to prioritize what to do next and then they worked together to create a better future. The leaders got involved in solving issues, and the people who work for them felt their leaders cared. All of that builds trust.

After listening, which is really important in our process, the leader of this organization went out on his own and made a response to the group about what he heard. He made a list of what changes he was personally committing to with the team, and the behaviors he was going to take responsibility for. He was vulnerable and said, "Here's what we are going to do about it." He admitted there were problems and that helped enormously. And once the people in the organization felt heard they said, "Okay, now it's a shared problem. We're not alone, so what are we doing to do about it?"

Being wrong, saying you are sorry, and saying you don't know are the hardest things for leaders to do; when you learn how, it's pivotal to building trust. There's a fine line, because you are still in charge and you don't want to instill panic, but you can say we are going to figure it out together.

By far the most inspiring leadership talk I ever heard was a speech given by Mike Murphy, a senior VP at Mars, Incorporated that was delivered to the top 140 global business leaders. In the speech, he was very honest and vulnerable. He described the process of being responsible as part of a leadership team for not only the brands and the related trust relationships with consumers as well as the success of the business but also the hopes and dreams, the passion for the products, and the people. "We want to articulate not only the company's history and business plans, but what will make it great in the future. We shared the trust that was given to us, and now we are sharing 'this gift' with you, as we realize we can't do this alone." It takes great courage and vulnerability on the leader's part to say, "I cannot do it alone."

Obviously, leaders need to focus on leading the organization, but they also need people. They can't do it all by themselves. But sometimes, focusing on people falls by the wayside and leaders forget. They start feeling like they have to do everything themselves, but no one can do it alone.

Get to Know Your People

Leaders can change this dynamic of wanting to go it alone in the workplace by getting to know the people who work for them. The best leaders I know engage with people, ask them about their kids, their health—they know what's going on with their employees and how they can help and support them. This has two benefits: 1. If the employee feels the leader genuinely cares about them as a person, they are much more willing to go the extra mile; 2. When the leader knows what's going on with the members of their team, they can anticipate what needs they will have.

> *"You can easily judge the character of a man by how he treats those who can do nothing for him."* GOETHE

So what's the DNA of the people who work for you?

D—Details: what do you know about them as people?

N—Needs: what drives them to do their best?

A—Approach: what is the best approach that you can use to help them work their best?

Treat everybody like they are somebody. Be flexible in your approach. Watch, listen, and adapt. Pay attention as employees and customers communicate how they want to be treated.

The best leaders understand it's not the Golden Rule in the workplace—"treat others as you would like to be treated"; instead, it's the Platinum Rule—"treat others as *they* would like to be treated."

How to Become a Conscious Leader

In order to become a conscious leader, the first step is to take a look at yourself. What do you think other people know about you as a person? Do people know what drives you? Do you know what drives you?

Then, you need to make an effort to both get to know your people and let them get to know you. This isn't always easy. I take time to create a new leader assimilation process with my clients to make the transition go smoother. This gives the team a clear understanding of the new leader's expectations, leadership style, and values. It also allows the leader to hear some things about the team and the organization that would take much longer without the process.

I use two sets of questions: one set of questions for the leader and another set for the staff.

I have a session with the leader and have them articulate their leadership style. Questions I might pose to them include:
- How would you describe your leadership style?
- How would you define success?
- What's your preferred method of communication?
- What motivates you?
- What do you see as the biggest obstacles for our team?
- What's your vision for this team?
- What are your weaknesses?
- What is your superpower?

Separately, I facilitate a conversation with the staff, who have generally been working together for a while, around things related to the leadership role and the business. Questions for the staff might be:
- What do we already know about (leader)?
- What don't we know but would like to know that would help us work together?
- What should (leader) know about us as a team?
- What do we need most from (leader) to be successful?
- What concerns do we have?

Business-related questions might be:
- What's working well for us?
- What are the key challenges we face?
- What's most critical to fix or prioritize?
- What are our big opportunities as a team?

The two groups then come back together and share the answers from their sessions. I always capture this visually because it's such a useful reference for the team and the leader afterward. It's a great learning experience and this conversation generates information about each other, which is a way of building trust. It wasn't the questions that matter, it was that they set up a structure for having a conversation and listening to each other. You can learn from any process of talking and listening. You don't even need a consultant. You just have to be willing to be curious and vulnerable.

To become a better, more conscious leader, you don't need to go to a mountaintop and meditate for a year; you can do all the learning you need to in your everyday context. Just be aware that everything you do matters. You create the employee experience, and you can change it once you are aware of it. Simple things make a difference. I had one client carry around a notebook to write down suggestions and ideas from employees so that he could actually remember them and act on them. That little act of doing so upped his trustworthiness.

Another very challenging yet necessary trust-building people skill is giving and receiving feedback. Often in the workplace, this is done via 360-degree feedback, but the best leaders are able to solicit feedback and give feedback effectively in real time. However, for most people, it's a very difficult skill to master. Why is this?

You already know I don't think surveys ever beat conversations, especially on sensitive subjects like performance and engagement. You have to be brave enough to have the conversation with people and ask them for feedback. A 360 survey could be a starting point. If I can't talk you out of it, have at it, spend the money. But realize that it's a starting point, not an endpoint. The flat feedback you get from a survey needs to have the richness of a real conversation. That is how you build engagement. It's like the difference between sending a mass mailer and calling. I feel you care about me and my opinion if you took the time to talk to me. But it's scary and takes time to feel comfortable doing it.

"Courage is never to let your actions be influenced by your fears."
ARTHUR KOESTLER

I listened to Sheila Heen, co-author of *Thanks for the Feedback,* who said that what makes feedback challenging is a juncture of two needs:

1. The need to learn and grow.
2. The need to be appreciated and loved as we are now.

Who has the best information about you? It's your team, and yet employees are often very afraid of giving honest feedback. As a leader, sometimes we're grateful and sometimes it's painful. Heen says feedback creates three triggers for us:

1. You're *wrong* (questioning the truth of what has been shared).
2. *Who* gave it (questioning the relationship with the person delivering the feedback).
3. I should be *better* (questioning the leader's own identity).

The best way to improve, of course, is through practice, and leaders need to create a safe space to allow feedback to come in to them. They need to deliver feedback in a way that is intended to improve someone's performance without tearing the person down—it has to be genuine and compassionate.

Strive to Become Your Best Self

Your self-development pays off for the organization. And you, as a leader, need to be working on yourself as part of your job. Who you are and how seriously you take your own development matters in engagement because it demonstrates to people that you are also continuously learning and trying to be the best version of yourself. We will talk later about developing your people; for right now, know that if you are not working on yourself, the culture of your organization won't encourage your employees even if you offer development programs.

Remind yourself and your organization that no one is finished developing. You're always going to be trying to be a better leader and learning about yourself and your people. You're always moving, like vision and strategy are always moving; you have to keep checking in to see if you are on track and learning and growing. What you do or what you develop is your own choice and it's all important. This impacts your people in ways that will change the culture of your group, your team, your organization.

For starters, you can work on some of the processes we talk about in this book for raising engagement, because they all call on leaders to become more present, more aware, and to listen better. See what skills stretch you and those are the first ones you can focus on. Just keep learning, keep making time, and keep showing your organization that you are hearing them.

13

The People Part

Leaders Who Listen

Leadership is about how you treat the people around you, which, by definition, means you must be both visible and available to them.

Tamara Christensen, design thinking expert, says, "I think listening is probably one of the most important and most undervalued communication skills. We'll have to focus on how to communicate, different ways to have conversations and ways to communicate and tell stories and things like that. Fundamentally, none of that works unless you have a good listener, unless you have someone who's actively engaged in absorbing and taking in what you're saying."

You may have heard the term "active listening." When I became a professional coach years ago, we learned that there are three levels of listening a coach can use:

Level 1: Listening to respond—when someone listens at this level, they are actually paying more attention to what's happening inside themselves and how they want to respond, rather than listening to the speaker. There is nothing wrong with this when someone asks a

"Success isn't about how much money you make; it's about the difference you make in people's lives."

MICHELLE OBAMA

question, like "Do you want to go out to lunch?" But if someone is expressing something that they are struggling with, focusing on ourselves is not being a good listener. An example of a Level 1 question might be "Can we find some other vendor?"

Level 2: Listening to understand—when someone is listening at this level, they are focused on the speaker, sometimes paraphrasing what the speaker is saying. An example of a Level 2 question might be "So, it sounds like you don't like the new upgrades?" In business, Levels 1 and 2 are the norm.

Level 3: Listening to be curious—when someone is listening at this level, they are not only paying attention to what is being said but noticing the body language, tone, and emotions of the speaker. As a speaker, you can tell when someone is genuinely listening to you at this level because they ask questions that come from a place of curiosity rather than knowledge. In coaching, we learn to pay attention to what's being said as well as what's not being said. An example of a Level 3 question might be "How did you become interested in marketing after a career in HR?"

Consider Disney, which understands that the secret to delighting their guests is to take great care of their employees. Disney leaders are encouraged to spend 60 per cent of their time with employees and guests, having conversations, listening to concerns, and taking steps to improve the experience for what they call internal customers (cast members) and external customers (guests).

In this way, Disney is doing what I do with clients—improving the employee experience, which, in turn, improves the customer experience. I know from my time with clients that the best way to improve your business is to have employees who feel aligned and engaged, and who can use their experience to delight the customers with whom they come in contact.

"It's amazing what you hear when you shut up and listen." DICK BARNES, CORPORATE VICE PRESIDENT (RETIRED), MARS, INCORPORATED

We demonstrate that we are listening by asking people for their opinions, thoughts and ideas. But the most important concept to remember:

Listen. Listen. Listen.
Listen more than you talk.
Speak less. Listen more.

"The quieter you become, the more you can hear." RAM DASS

Listening means creating space for important conversations to happen. Listening means allowing pauses in the conversation, being conscious of whose voice has the most airtime. I often describe this to groups as big share of voice and little share of voice—the leader should be the smaller talk bubble, not the larger one.

Asking questions like "I wonder…" and "I'm curious…" helps draw out people to contribute to the conversations. The wisdom of many exceeds that of the leader or any one individual. And when you empower one to contribute, you encourage the rest to engage. When your organization is empowered, the employees help make the company successful.

Listening, engaging, and improving your employees' experience are strategies that serve your bottom line and don't come out of old school, top-down strategy, but out of a strategy based on empathy and compassion. It used to be that when we talked about business strategy, what we were really talking about was slightly updated, top-down, military-style ideas about how the world works. This was true of just about every company anywhere. The tide has turned, and people are realizing that this style of leadership isn't working anymore.

It's clear to anyone paying attention to Millennials and Gen Z folks that they're not going to want to watch pontificating leaders. They are demanding conversational leaders. What does that look like in real life?

How to Lead with Your Ears

There's more to listening than waiting for your turn to talk. Without people skills, there's high turnover, low morale, low productivity, and unhealthy internal competition—summed up as low engagement. The experience of the employees suffers and everyone feels that the culture is not working.

Questions to ask yourself to start thinking about conversational leadership:

- Where do you find yourself spending the majority of your energy and attention?
- When you walk away, how do you feel (energized or depleted)?

Leaders often find themselves dreading interactions with the people who deplete their energy: the highly disengaged, low performers. Yet, if these employees are not dealt with, it does two things: it saps the energy of the leader and it de-incentivizes engaged employees. Consider the alternative: if the leader addresses the low performers, there's more energy to focus on the positive employees. And the low performers, through conversation, may become big contributors. You don't know why they are suffering until you ask.

A client, a female leader from America, worked at a manufacturing plant in Prague. She had both a language barrier and a cultural barrier to overcome. The employees were not happy about their work or the organization's leaders. Cultural sensitivities made them not trust a leader from another country. She made a real effort to listen through some really hard feedback. The people who were giving the input were so upset that they were quite intimidating.

This amazing leader stuck through it and kept listening and kept getting the feedback about what the issues were. She knew some of the issues were that her new direct reports were using a command and control leadership style. She listened and committed to making some real change. She and her HR leader really held the space for the discussion to happen even though people were very mad.

Through our process, the employees had some real breakthroughs on the suggestions they were making for change. Once they knew they were being heard, they realized they could help solve the problems. They began suggesting really great improvements.

We spent two days working the actions that were suggested, with employees and leaders together talking through what the issues were. The employees felt heard and things began to shift.

I stayed in touch with her and the feedback was that people saw real listening and then real action because she followed through. What she did made a real impression on the people who worked for her. She came through a tough situation to be a leader who changed the culture of that factory and the experience of the people who worked there. All by being willing to listen.

Reducing Misconceptions: Contact Hypothesis

There's a concept in sociology called the contact hypothesis, which refers to the belief that prejudices can be lessened or eliminated by direct contact between groups. In manufacturing organizations, there's often a sharp divide between office and factory workers. Because they have little contact with each other, they form opinions and biases about the other group. To get over those biases, listening is key.

As a leader, you are the person who needs to model listening. It's about you seeking to understand them—whoever the "them" is to your "us." That listening builds trust and shows interest. It isn't about you anymore, no matter how hard it seems, even if you don't speak the language and you are scared and it's rough.

Shared Humanity

We hear of examples every day of people hurting other people. At the 2017 TEDxUCSD event, I was struck by speaker Neil Senturia's talk, "Shared Humanity." He talked about an exercise he participated in with entrepreneurs-in-training (EITs), where they went into a prison to work with prisoners before their release. The EITs lined up facing a line of prisoners, and the facilitator drew a line of tape on the floor between them. The facilitator then posed a series of statements, and if you could answer "yes," you stepped onto the line. The statements began simply and gradually become more difficult, like "my parents paid for college," "I've lived in poverty," and "I've lost a child." The commonality surprised both groups. Senturia said it reminded everyone of their shared humanity—for many of the EITs, the gratitude for their good fortune and privilege that allowed them to make different choices.

Shortly after a deadly white supremacist rally in Charlottesville, Virginia, there was a rally in Berkeley, California. PRX (Public Radio Exchange) reporter Al Letson saw an alt-right man fall to the ground, and some Antifa protesters beating him.

"When I glanced to my left I saw, you know, a *mass* of people just coming off the lawn toward this guy, and I don't know—I just, I thought they were going to kill him. And I just didn't want anybody to die," Letson says. "And I just put my body down on top of his, in the hopes that they would not hit me."

Letson jumped on top of the guy to protect him, because, he says, he didn't want anyone to get hurt. When he was interviewed about the incident, he said, "It doesn't matter if he doesn't see my humanity, what matters to me is that I see his. What he thinks about me and all of that, like—my humanity isn't dependent upon that."

Over and over in my work, I hear stories of employees whose bosses don't even know their name or just walk by. Let's face it—we all despise being ignored, overlooked, rejected, or treated like we're invisible. Especially with more and more technology in our everyday lives that disconnects us, people crave actual human connection. Powerful leaders know how to connect and engage with people. They know that we are all more similar than different. And they know that when push comes to shove, like Al Letson, they would do anything for their employees.

Really Seeing People

Ashanti Branch, a Stanford d.school (Design School) fellow, spoke to a group of young men, sharing a story of when he was a high school teacher. When he would pass students or other teachers in the hallway, he wouldn't just politely say, "How are you?" but would really deliver these words with intention. He would stop and make eye contact as he said it, because he wanted to communicate not only that he was truly interested in their answer, but to let them know that he really *saw* them in that moment. He said it was a very powerful thing to do and would sometimes catch people off guard, but people gradually became appreciative of his genuineness and compassion for them. This story has stayed with me, and I now consciously stop and wait for the answer rather than just continuing to walk by.

He made an impact because he listened. People were uncomfortable and caught off guard because they were not used to someone being fully present. Imagine the difference this could make to the people with whom you work.

How to Listen Like a Leader

Celeste Headlee, in her TED talk "10 Ways to Have a Better Conversation," says she grew up in a family where people would drop by; as a result, she met many interesting people. Based on this, she grew up interested in people and is always prepared to be amazed. Her ten rules for listening:

1. Don't multitask. Be present.
2. Don't pontificate—you always have something to learn.
3. Ask good questions, use who-what-when-where-why.
4. Check your thoughts—they will come in and out; let them go.
4. If you don't know, SAY you don't know.
5. Don't equate your experience with others—it's not about you.
6. Don't be condescending, don't repeat.
7. Forget the details.
8. LISTEN.
9. Be brief. In fact, Celeste quotes her sister's sage advice: "A good conversation is like a miniskirt: short enough to retain interest, but long enough to cover the subject."

At the W Hotel, a best practice to engage employees is called "Open Mic," where they have employees share what's good, what's working, and what needs improvement. These meetings create an atmosphere of sharing and conversation around how to continuously improve. We will talk more in future chapters about the process I use, which is listening based, but any process you put in place to listen will improve your employees' experience of your culture.

"Courage is what it takes to stand up and speak; courage is also what it takes to sit down and listen." WINSTON CHURCHILL

One-on-One Communication

There are many popular books and workshops on topics like "courageous conversations," "fierce conversations," and "crucial conversations." Their prevalence demonstrates the great need for improvement in the way we talk to one another. I find people's feelings about communication are deeply rooted in family and childhood, where they (most often) saw poor communication. As a result, they don't know how to have an effective, positive interaction when there's potential disagreement or conflict.

Powerful conversations have the potential to create change, but they must be handled well for this to happen. They require such things as:
- Responding rather than reacting.
- The ability to stop and think.
- Acknowledging, asking, and inquiring.
- Being curious.
- Being courageous.
- Using "and" rather than "but."
- Considering: what is the courageous question that will move the conversation forward?

Be mindful of the dangers of triangulation, which occurs when I have a problem with Mary so I go to Peter to tell him my problems with Mary. This does not help Mary, who never gets to hear what I'm upset about. It doesn't help Peter either, who's now burdened with my problem but is powerless to resolve it. It only helps me momentarily release some frustration. No one wins. Instead, create an environment where people are encouraged to:
- Say what they mean.
- Mean what they say.
- Say it to the right person.

Words Matter

The words and the language that a leader uses are critical. I've heard leaders use powerless phrases like "try to," "might," and "could," which send powerful messages about the low level of commitment. I've also heard employees referred to as "hourlies" or "temps"—I try to picture how unmotivated I would feel if I were called either of these titles, feeling like I could be let go at any time.

The most underused phrases that can make the biggest difference in leadership and in life? "Thank you" and "I'm sorry." Be generous with these phrases and see how life changes for you and how people react to you.

Design Thinking and Leadership

In Chapter 5 I explained the concept of design thinking, but how does design thinking relate to leadership? As it turns out, empathy, a key leadership skill, is also the basis for innovation through design thinking.

According to design thinking expert Tamara Christensen, "Leadership has undergone a radical transformation. Last century leadership was about increasing performance and eliminating waste. This century's leadership is much less about telling people what to do and measuring performance and more to do with tapping into the capabilities of the people who work for you so that they can deliver solutions to problems no one has ever faced." Translation: as a modern leader, your job is to see the potential of your people and draw it out.

This sounds very much like the kind of leadership we are talking about when we talk about improving the experience for employees on every level and in everything they do.

"Just because it could be worse doesn't mean it's not our job to make it better." KAT COLE, FORMER PRESIDENT OF CINNABON

Traditional thinking manager	Design thinking leader
Mainly verbal, uses diagrams and tables	Mainly visual, uses sketching, whiteboarding, and prototyping to convey ideas
Quick interpretation of a situation	Intense observation and wondering, challenges stereotypical perceptions
Mainly rational and objective	Emotional and rational at the same time, subjective
Looks for "correct" answers	Understands failure is part of the process
Leads by organizing and planning	Comfortable with ambiguity and uncertainty
Customer-driven—considers what clients want for social status	Empathic and human-driven—understands people's needs and dreams
Principally individual	Principally collaborative

We've all had bad leaders and good leaders. The good ones, as a group, are empathetic and they listen. Think about leaders you have had in the past who inspired you because they do things right. Remember how that felt and what went into it. Did they listen, care about your success? Did they want better for you? Did they take action to support your job?

Whatever they did, you can do, too, and you should do it to pay forward the good leadership you've experienced. It may seem amorphous right now, in the way culture did when we first started talking about it in the first part of the book. But you became an expert on feeling culture and you can become an expert here on leadership, too. I will take you through the process in Part Six.

14

The Continuous Journey
of Leadership

EADERSHIP IS A continuous journey—there is no end point. That's both the good news and the bad news. The good news is you are always improving; the bad news is you are always improving. And the questions I have learned leaders need to ask themselves are:

- Am I learning?
- Am I demonstrating my learning in meetings and encounters with my people?

There have been many debates over the years about whether leaders are naturally born with leadership skills or whether they can be taught. Over and over, research and stories show that while some people possess natural leadership skills from the start, most people can develop their skillset to be a great leader. Like all things, it takes hard work and practice, a willingness to make mistakes, receive feedback, and learn to be a great leader.

"The heaviness of being successful was replaced by the lightness of being a beginner again."

STEVE JOBS

"Feedback" is a key word here—the willingness to learn from both the positive and the negative and to create a culture where it's good to help people learn and change. Founder and CFO of Lenati Courtney Klein told me that for her, feedback is a learning tool: "One of the things I do is tell people how I like to receive feedback. My favorite framework is: 'Here's where you did really well, here's where you've done the most, and here are your opportunities for growth.' So, it's all really positive and the opportunities for growth shouldn't be negative things. And I think it's really important to be really specific and actionable. Our CEO gives me one nugget of feedback at a time. And I think, 'Okay, I can do something with that. I can definitely do something with that.'"

But leadership is a journey—there's no end point. You are always learning new ways to do things, new approaches to working with people. The journey begins the first day you work with another person and ends the day you stop interacting with people. It's not about having a formal role, but rather about paying attention.

We all spend our days and weeks focused on the *doing* side of things—that's where to-do lists and calendars focus our energy. But to be an effective leader, you have to spend some time on the *being* side—how you are living your life moment to moment.

- What is your purpose?
- What vision do you have for yourself?
- What are your goals?

> *"If you don't design your own life plan, chances are you'll fall into someone else's plan. And guess what they have planned for you? Not much."* JIM ROHN

Leaders must make a personal commitment to continuous learning and development, which happens in a variety of ways: classroom learning, feedback, coaching (either from peers, a mentor, or a professional coach). Here are some areas for leaders to develop awareness of their impact: time management, meetings, coaching, listening, and setting the tone for culture and employee experience.

While at Lenati, I asked the team questions about leadership and culture, and they drew a strong correlation between how the leaders behave and the tone of the culture and the employee experience. If leaders support their employees' growth, listen and learn from them, and take feedback well, the whole culture becomes more productive.

One of the newer members of Lenati happens to be my new college graduate daughter, Kylah, who recently did a presentation at a "lunch and learn" session. She presented on economic growth in China. Several of the senior leaders I interviewed mentioned the talk and how it exemplified what is great about their work culture—the focus on learning and development at all levels.

You have to develop yourself and your people. You cannot depend on "job training," as that should be a given. Development is a broader level of learning. Don't limit people to their field. Let them learn in other fields and you should, too. People's desire and willingness to be curious will allow them to expand their role and grow into new jobs. We will talk in Chapter 20 about creating this learning culture for your employees; here we want to focus on you.

If you do this yourself, you will be a better leader.

You can check yourself very simply by asking, "Are the people in my organization (including me) learning and growing?" We talked earlier about modeling for the organization the very skills and traits you want your team to have, and this focus on developing yourself and always learning is a prime one to model.

Learning to Manage Busy-ness

Everyone these days answers "How are you?" with "I'm SO BUSY!" Is it really shameful to *not* have a full calendar? Take my dear eighty-five-year-old mother, who spent the last five years of her life in assisted living. I would visit her and ask her how she was. "I'm very busy!"

Really? Because if we can't slow down to smell the roses at eighty-five, when can we slow down?

The trouble is we are all working on computer time. We were sold a promise that when technology came along, it would automate tasks and we would have more time, but instead, we work on 24/7 time (that phrase didn't exist when I was growing up). And there's a great deal of confusion between being busy versus accomplishing things we want to accomplish. A lack of time indicates we aren't prioritizing, managing pressures, assessing, and adjusting as needed.

Technology was touted to be our friend when it was introduced. It was going to save us time! Create more freedom! We went from working on agrarian time (by the sun and moon) to industrial to now a technology timeframe. Greg McKeown, author of *Essentialism*, says, "Technology is a poor master but a great student." What's not factored in is that machines do not need to sleep and recharge. They don't have families or friends. They don't eat. And they truly work 24 hours a day, 7 days a week, 365 days a year, without stopping. As humans, we cannot keep up with this pace. And yet it's up to us to set the limits—the machines aren't going to do it. We've institutionalized the drama that's needed to get things done. Now we just feel we need to work harder, faster.

Are you ever completely caught up? Yeah, me neither.

If a leader isn't focusing on the right things—culture, learning, development, listening—and is, instead, focusing on time and the amount of work people should be doing, creating a culture of busyness, then they end up with teams and people who have no time to get good at what they do.

I've been paying a lot of attention to the topic of busy-ness lately. I heard McKeown speak to a group of leaders at Cisco about this phenomenon he called "The Busy-ness Bubble," where being busy has become a badge of honor people wear to show how important they are. I was recently shamed for not being busy when I responded to someone that I was relaxed. "I'd love to know your secret!" he responded sarcastically. McKeown shared that before the Industrial Revolution, people used to use the word "priority."

Singular. One.

Since we've industrialized, we have multiple priorities, competing demands, and lack of focus. No wonder we're so tired!

Let's face it. We live in a hyper-connected world, where you can get information all the time, anytime, anywhere. How many of us sleep with our phone right next to our beds, claiming we need it for the alarm. Really? Didn't we used to have a device for that called a clock?

There's an addiction factor to busy-ness, just like there's a proven addiction to mobile devices. Addictions trigger a brain response and a release of dopamine; like drug addictions, they sometimes require more in order to get the same effect. A packed schedule makes us feel important, like we matter. It strokes our ego.

I was talking about this to a colleague recently, and he said, "I wonder what people mean by using the word *busy*?" Great question. There is healthy busy—working on things that matter, feeling like you are making a contribution. And then there's unhealthy busy—feeling overwhelmed and overloaded by too much to do.

> *"Being busy costs you too much—your health, unbalanced well-being, work/life disharmony, inefficient use of time, meaningless relationships, etc."* MICHAEL SEAVER, "BEING BUSY DOESN'T MEAN SUCCESS"

McKeown talks about the problem of being successful: you are rewarded with more options and opportunities. Now go back to that ego thing. Now more is better. And soon you are drowning in more, and you go from healthy-busy to unhealthy-busy to addicted to over-whelmed. Not good. And not productive either—you go from doing things well to just doing enough to get by. And you may remember Jim Rohn's quote from earlier: if you don't prioritize your life, someone else will. McKeown is a proponent of what he calls "the disciplined pursuit of less." Disciplined because it takes work and effort to stop saying "yes" to things.

> *"If you can't say 'no,' then your 'yes' means nothing."* PETER BLOCK

I tried this approach of creating personal focus. McKeown suggests a quarterly offsite with yourself to be clear on what you want to achieve. I looked at all the things I wanted (or needed) to get done, and chose two business priorities and one personal priority (hey, I *aspire* to be focused. I didn't say I was there yet). A month into it I felt really good. I was tracking my progress and feeling productive. And things were happening! It seems focus is really a good thing.

Sadly, people are so busy they're losing a sense of what it means to be connected with other humans (not the technology that we cradle). I read a *New York Times* article by Christine Porath called "No Time to Be Nice at Work," which gave an overview of the impact of constant rudeness to people in the workplace. The article talked about stress and the relationship to well-being as a growing topic in the world of engagement.

What does the incivility of being "too busy" look like to employees? According to Porath, it's probably the things you see every day: people texting, internet surfing, taking calls during meetings or while they are in conversations, not really listening when others are talking, and, sometimes even more overt, like openly mocking people, blaming people for problems and taking full credit, as well as reminders of one's role and title.

And how does this rudeness affect people? Porath indicates people tend to lose focus, make errors, and are less creative. As well, they are less likely to contribute and lose their conviction. There are also health implications, as being in a constant state of stress keeps our adrenalin turned up—what our distant relatives experienced when they were threatened by a mastodon or a saber-toothed tiger. But this state raises our blood pressure and depletes our adrenal system. Cardiovascular disease and a variety of illnesses become the inevitable yet potentially preventable outcome.

And yet, it doesn't take *any* extra time to be nice! It just takes the conscious awareness to do so. And in so doing, you remind the people with whom you work that you care, are listening, and can lead. Not a bad outcome.

The way out of this culture of busy-ness is leaders focusing on their own development, focusing on their culture, and listening to the people who work for them. For as long as I've been working, people have complained about wanting more work-life balance. Here is my wake-up call: no one is going to make this happen for you. You have to create it yourself.

It will be you and only you who sets the boundaries of time and what you get involved in, what you prioritize. If you want to lead, this is a place you are going to need to be brutally honest with yourself and take a look at the example you are setting and the tone of your organization.

Digital Detox Quiz

- Do you use your phone as an alarm clock? (Y/N)
- On average, do you eat at your desk or with your laptop/cell phone open? (Y/N)
- For how many meals a day are you 100 per cent screen-free?
- Do you take calls, texts, peruse the web, or answer emails on the toilet? (Y/N)
- Do you text and walk? (Y/N)
- Do you multi-task? (Y/N)
- How many tabs do you typically have open on your computer?
- Do you find yourself reaching for your phone and checking your email even if you didn't get alerts for new messages? (Y/N)
- Do you share photos, updates, or check-in on social media? (Y/N)
- How many times a day?
- Do you use cell phones or computers in the bedroom? (Y/N)
- Have you ever checked your email in the middle of the night? (Y/N)
- Do you ever feel anxious when you don't have your phone with you? (Y/N)
- On average, how many hours a day do you spend staring at a screen? (Phone, computer, TV, tablet for work, leisure, pleasure.)
- How many friends do you have on Facebook? Twitter? Instagram? Snapchat? Others?
- When was the last time you went 48 hours without your phone, media, or digital devices?

- What's the first thing you do when you wake up and the last thing you do before bed?

  Device-Specific Questions (you'll need your phone for this part)
- How many unread messages do you currently have?
- How many text messages remain unresolved?
- How many voicemails do you need to check?

Check in with yourself: how do you feel right now, after completing this quiz?

Meetings Can Create Engagement

Another way in which leaders can grow and lead better is through holding better meetings. Everyone dreads meetings, citing many things that make them so terrible. I actually wrote a whole book about internal meetings, and here were my Top 5 reasons people find meetings dysfunctional (from my book *To Meet or NOT to Meet?*):

1. There are no clear outcomes.
2. They are a waste of time.
3. The wrong people are in the meeting.
4. People are disorganized and unprepared.
5. There seems to be a "wild west" mentality all around.

I am a big proponent of meetings, but only if they're well organized and well run.

Meetings are probably one of the most obvious ways leaders can communicate, recognize, and connect with the people who work for them—in other words, create a high level of engagement. In a team setting, leaders can get to know team members better, communicate key updates, encourage the sharing of ideas, and acknowledge progress, completed projects, and individual accomplishments. It's possible to have great meetings—but you have to work at it.

You can run great meetings when the face-to-face contact is necessary and you can know when to leave people alone to work. In fact, you can also set the tone for your meetings so that they are productive and based on good listening.

Control Yourself

One last thing as a leader you might want to think about is to be on top of things enough, contained enough, and self-aware enough not to run around saying, "The sky is falling!" You need to show up composed—that's half the battle. You don't actually need to always know what to do. You do need to know what *not* to do!

Years ago, I took a coaching class, and I was carpooling with my friend Robin—it was an hour drive each way. There was a day when she was driving and I was meeting my husband at the symphony; we hit traffic and I was very worried as we were running late. Robin turned to me and said, "You have all the time you need." I was immediately calmed by her words. It's not that she told me how to solve the problem, but reminded me of what was in my control and what was not—and that was life-changing. I have repeated it to myself, clients, and friends many times since.

Don't make things stressful for yourself or other people.

All the research and studies have shown that the biggest impact on people is their direct manager. How you lead your people has the biggest impact on their feelings about work. You are their direct link to the culture of the organization, you create their experience and their feelings about their job, and you have a big impact on their work day. In fact, you have an impact on how they feel when they leave work and go home to their family and their community. The ripple effect is much bigger than you realize.

If you grow and learn and try to get better as a leader you are modeling the way for people, modeling the behaviors you want them to have. In all the above things—business, stress, development and growth, culture—you need to model the way your organization should live them.

15

Corporate Social Responsibility (CSR)

AN AMAZING THING happened in January 2018. BlackRock CEO Larry Fink, representing one of the largest investment firms in the world, sent out a letter to all of their CEOs. The letter, titled "A Sense of Purpose," told them that their responsibility isn't only to deliver profits but also to make "a positive contribution to society." Instead of the preoccupation with short-term profits, he outlined contributions as a focus on "investments in employee development, innovation, and capital expenditures that are necessary for longer-term growth." Fink addressed the CEOs as leaders responsible for making the world a better place, beyond just corporate profits. "Without a sense of purpose, no company can achieve its full potential."

One of the ways in which companies show their values and behaviors is by their sense of responsibility not just to their shareholders but the world. In the last chapter we talked about leaders modeling behaviors to change employee experience, and this is doubly true of companies who model larger responsibility. Let's not just look at short-term shareholder value but long-term stakeholder values.

"Corporate social responsibility is a hard-edged business decision. Not because it is a nice thing to do or because people are forcing us to do it … because it is good for our business."

NIALL FITZGERALD, FORMER CEO, UNILEVER

These ways of reaching the communities you work in and live in and participate in begin to bring engagement to your stakeholders.

Contributing to the Community

For every company there's a community, or several. There's the local community where you work and have your offices, there's the greater community including your suppliers, and there's the world in which your customers live and have their lives. How do you include all of these in your sense of responsibility? The philosophy is if we take care of our ecosystem, that will also increase shareholder value; it may not happen short term, but it will in a long-term way.

MARS Mars, Incorporated did a lot of work in Brazil, and at one point there was an issue with the growth of the cocoa plants there. They could have done a lot of things to solve the problem in the short term—from switching vendors or parts of the world to demanding it be fixed. What they did instead was to create something that would help the situation, not just for their own good but for the good of the farmers: they put money, people, and time into helping solve the problem with and for the farmers and the communities instead of abandoning them. This was also in keeping with the Mars Mutuality Principle of acting as a good corporate citizen to minimize the impact on the environment and to use the natural resources of our planet wisely and efficiently.

It has been interesting to watch the trend of corporations making a shift from just focusing on their bottom line or shareholder value to contributing to their community. Corporate Social Responsibility (CSR) is a business approach that contributes to sustainable development by delivering economic, social, and environmental benefits for all stakeholders. CSR is a very broad concept that addresses many topics such as human rights, corporate governance, health and safety, environmental effects, working conditions, and contribution to economic development. The purpose of CSR is to drive change toward sustainability.

For example, many companies like Starbucks and Mars work hard to source their raw materials (in this case, coffee and chocolate) from sustainable growers. Mars goes further in terms of reaching out to their suppliers and teaching them sustainable farming techniques. Unilever has an initiative called the "sustainable tea program," where they partner with the Rainforest Alliance and aim to source all of their Lipton and PG tips tea bags from Rainforest Alliance–certified farms. The Rainforest Alliance certification offers farms a way to differentiate their products as being socially, economically, and environmentally sustainable.

Triple Bottom Line

Triple Bottom Line (TBL) refers to the demands that a company's responsibility lies with stakeholders rather than shareholders. In this case, "stakeholders" refers to anyone who is influenced, either directly or indirectly, by the actions of the firm, which includes employees, customers, suppliers, local residents, government agencies, and creditors. While this is enforced in the public sector, it has gained a lot of traction in the private sector, where companies want to look at their performance through a broader lens than just shareholder value.

Spreading the message that the company isn't just about profits, but about contributing to the communities they exist in, has helped companies succeed. What's wonderful about these programs is they don't have to cost a lot in order to make an impact.

Zappos, for example, has a number of CSR programs that contribute to their local communities. For example, they do a program called Zappos for Good, which is a speaker series where they sell tickets to the public and then profits are donated to charities.

Expressworks, a consulting firm based in Dallas, Texas, conducted a corporate retreat in Baja, Mexico. In the planning, attendees

were asked to bring clothing to donate to the local community. They also conducted a team-building exercise that used canned goods, which afterward were donated to the local community. Finally, they invited local artisans onsite for an evening event, where the artisans could interact with the attendees and attendees could learn about the process of making the goods and buy them to take home.

MARS Mars, Incorporated often has offsite conferences or team retreats, where part of the expectation is that they will connect with the local community of their event and deliver some positive impact. This comes in the form of building, donating, or organizing. At one event I facilitated, the leader had organized a team building event at a local food bank. We broke into two teams and "competed" to prepare Thanksgiving packages that would be delivered to the local community in Chicago. This not only delivered a useful service to the community but was also a great way to create community within the team! This activity cost nothing but the time it took to schedule it with the food bank.

All of these are examples of modeling care and responsibility: leaders modeling it for their people and companies modeling it for the world.

"We make a living by what we get,
but we make a life by what we give."

WINSTON CHURCHILL

The Employee Experience Lifecycle

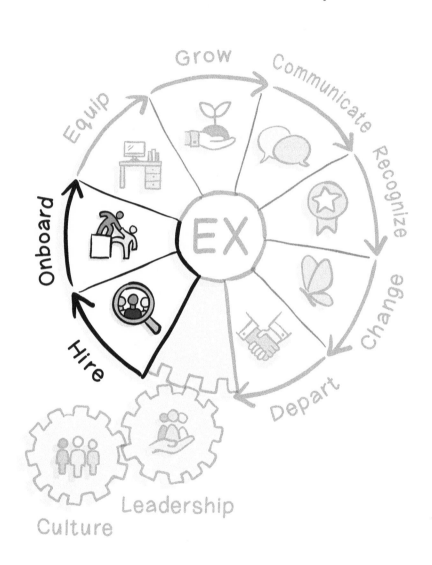

4

Processes That Welcome Employees

The Employee Experience Lifecycle

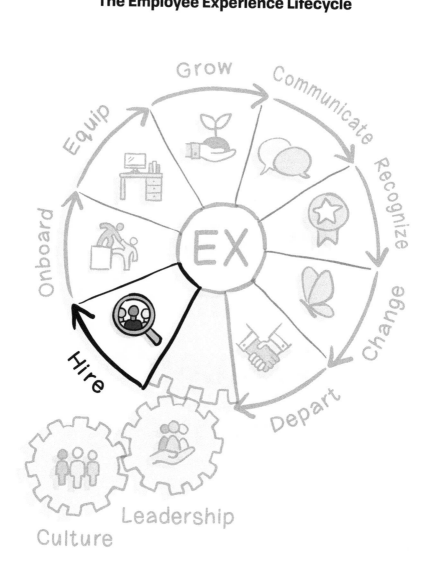

16

Getting the Right People in the Door

CAN'T TELL YOU how many times I've heard the expression about the bus that Jim Collins popularized in his landmark book. He's passionate about making sure the engaged employees are in the right jobs, and the disengaged are quickly walked to the door.

Collins is not the only voice in this conversation. I was fortunate enough to meet Adam Grant, author of *Give and Take* and the youngest tenured professor at Wharton, who goes further, saying you must weed out the "takers," those who take without giving much back, and seek out the "givers," those who enjoy helping others without strings attached.

In my interviews with Lenati, one of the things they talked about extensively was their hiring practice. They hired for the kind of company they wanted to have—particularly their young hires, whom they saw already had a learning mindset. Pam Spier, Head of Client Delivery, spoke about her hiring practices and said they hire for cultural fit, because the tone and the feeling of the organization

"Get the right people on the bus, the wrong people off the bus, and then the right people in the right seats."

JIM COLLINS, *GOOD TO GREAT*

were crucial to their success. She said that one of the ways she knew this concept succeeded was that friendships grew between people who started working together. She called it "start date friends" and that was always a sign of great fit.

Charles Tragesser, Lenati's Talent Acquisition Manager, told me when they hire, "The candidates are being interviewed by people who are doing the work. And we always level it up one level, so in interviewing someone for an analyst position, we can use a consultant or senior consultant to do the interview. If we're hiring for senior consultant we need a manager. But, in every case, this is someone who intimately knows our work. The big question is: would you want this person on your team? Also, everybody here is so wicked smart so that the first pass is always about culture fit and thinking."

I've worked with many companies over the years who have practically worn out the expression "war on talent" and a desire to become the "employer of choice." The first expression, "war on talent," is all about competition in the marketplace for employees who will fit in to the company's culture, have the skills needed to help the company succeed, and the right attitude to be a team player. While there's obviously not an actual war, there are just great choices and not so great choices of people to fit into your culture and organization.

"Employer of choice" means each company is vying to stand out amongst other successful companies, using not only competitive salaries but also meaningful benefits to potential employees. Many companies work hard to create a strong employer brand to stand out from their competitors. Hiring good people is essential to creating a successful company, and engaged people are likely to attract even more good people. However, if you are doing it right, the people who fit choose you.

Hiring can be one of the most effective ways to design the culture you want to have. This means there must be a conscious awareness of the desired culture and what qualities people must possess in order to get there; generally, companies focus on the qualifications of the people they hire rather than the attitudes of potential employees. Unfortunately, focusing only on qualifications won't create a very successful company.

Hiring for Attitude

> *"Hire for attitude and train for skills."* BILL TAYLOR,
> *HARVARD BUSINESS REVIEW*

You can train for a lot of things, but you can't train a person's personality and attitude. So it's critical that you look beyond the skills that someone shows up with to who they are as a person. Look at Southwest Airlines as a great example—they hire looking for a "Warrior Spirit" that they know fits with how they want their employees to act on the job. Here are some best practices at companies you might know.

 Zappos has a unique hiring process; they have nearly 30,000 applications for about 450 openings annually. There aren't individual job postings, which Zappos considers too transactional; instead, there's a social network called the Zappos Insider Program. Anyone interested in working for the company can join the program and network with current employees. Recruiters monitor the interactions, focusing on proactive sourcing, and can pull from the program when a position becomes available.

If you get through the screening process and are lucky enough to be invited for an interview, there will actually be two interviews: one with the hiring manager and a team to determine if you have the skillset needed, and a second interview with HR, who is looking primarily at cultural fit—you have to pass both interviews to be hired.

Zappos is also very thoughtful about how they handle candidates they don't hire. In line with their cultural values of "build open and honest relationships with communication" and "deliver WOW through service," each unsuccessful applicant hears back about results of the process. Zappos considers it to be respectful, and interviewed candidates will receive feedback to help them grow. As you can imagine, this is a great process for their employer brand.

 At Google, employees are hired for capability and learning ability rather than expertise. Google looks for curious, smart people who are open to new ideas. They don't believe it's in the company's best interest to ever compromise on the "hiring bar," and they'd rather kiss a lot of frogs to get the right people in the door; they realize the high cost of not hiring well to their current employees and the corporate culture overall. As with many things at Google, the process is very objective, with data and committees driving the decisions rather than individuals. For example, the hiring manager does not make the final hiring decision, and things like "intuition" do not factor into their formula. But as they say, they are hiring people who fit. They call it "Googly," as in "Are you Googly enough?" They know that getting the right people in the door matters.

 The Ritz-Carlton has a genuine commitment to making sure they get the right people in the door. In fact, they would say they don't "hire" individuals but instead "select" ladies and gentlemen who are aligned with the values and philosophy of the Ritz-Carlton culture. They look for attributes like pride, ownership, and passion, as these qualities cannot be trained or taught.

Apple

 At Apple's retail stores, which provide most of the customer-facing activities for the company, hiring is key. In his book, *The Apple Experience*, Carmine Gallo goes behind the company's retail operation to uncover some of the elements that make it so successful. Hiring is critical, and they don't hire for technical knowledge nearly as much as for personality—10 per cent of the weight is on the former while 90 per cent rests on the latter.

 At Disney, the happiest place on Earth, you can apply online, where you will find the Disney vision, culture, and appearance guidelines outlined for potential future cast members. You can apply in person at something called a "casting call," for "roles" (not jobs). At an in-person event, you will see a video explaining the corporation's history, the appearance requirements, scheduling, and transportation guidelines. When interviewing, Disney looks for people who fit their corporate culture.

Hire Slowly. Fire Quickly.

By hiring slowly, you are thoughtful rather than just hiring anyone who may or may not fit in with your culture. Firing quickly does not mean knee-jerk reaction, but when you recognize that someone isn't a good fit, they can do more damage to a functioning team than you realize. Here are some good reasons I've seen, from an engagement perspective, to let them go sooner rather than later:

- When you really come to the conclusion that it's not a good fit, it's almost guaranteed that others have realized this awhile ago.
- If you procrastinate, others won't see you as a committed leader with conviction.
- Disengaged people are like cancer—their negativity can affect others.
- As the old saying goes, "A chain (or in this case, a team) is only as strong as its weakest link."

Netflix considers their employees with something they call a "Keeper's Test." Which of your people, if they told you they were leaving, would you fight hard to keep?

Leaders are key in hiring the right people. One of my favorite expressions was voiced by my client Brian Abrahamson, who said, "Look for tens and potential tens. Sevens don't hire tens, they hire fives and sevens." This took me a few minutes to unravel, but when I did it was a powerful message about confident leadership and being comfortable enough to have people look better than you for the betterment of the organization. When sevens hire fives and sevens, there's a spiraling cycle down to mediocrity. If you hire the best, they will hire the best and so on.

Getting the Right People Is Up to You

Laszlo Bock says getting the right people in the door is on you. It is your process of hiring, so if you don't get good people, then figure that out early. Have really good processes so you can see engagement fairly early on if you know what to look for. The potential hire needs to show that they are an engaged person and the process needs to bring the right people through the funnel.

Engagement and employee experience are a product of the people who work with you. It's everyone's responsibility to create the culture they want to work in; it's the company's responsibility to bring the people who can do that. You can hire for engagement, you can fire for not having it, but you want to find the people who can create it and draw in others to do the same.

The Employee Experience Lifecycle

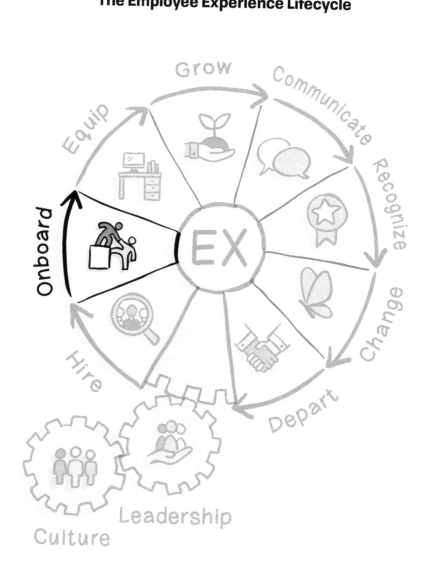

17

Treat People Right from the Start

ANY YEARS AGO, I heard a talk called "The Stupid People." In the talk, the speaker shared how, because most of us are raised to be nice, when the doorbell rings or there's a knock, we automatically open the door, often without making any attempt to find out who is on the other side. When we do this, we remove the biggest and only barrier we have to create safety: our front door. Her message was to use good sense rather than politeness when opening a door, and to teach our children, who are even more vulnerable, to do the same, so we only allow those we want into our homes.

Hiring is similar, in that a lot of work should be done up front to get the right people to the door, with an eventual invitation given only to the right person to come in. For starters, the process of hiring a new employee, getting them to the door, is very expensive. On average, it can cost 30–400 per cent of an employee's annual salary to replace someone depending on their level; every change creates uncertainty amongst co-workers as well as productivity and morale issues. It is simply not worth it to open the door to anyone

"Onboarding is the perfect opportunity to make a positive, lasting impression on a new hire. It really is the honeymoon phase for new employees. They've just agreed to come and work for a new company, and they are prepared to be wowed. But the employer must deliver."

BEN EUBANKS, UPSTARTHR

asks them how it's going. And on Anniversary Day 365, the group rejoins one last time to celebrate their first year at the company. This establishes a great employee experience where people feel well cared for and important.

 New hires at Disney spend a day at Disney University doing something called "Traditions." Disney trainers share stories about the past, present, and future of the Disney organization. As well, Disney traditions and values are shared through storytelling, examples, and activities. The goal for the company is to build pride in the brand and learn about the culture and the values. It works well for Disney, as they have a reputation for the best customer service and employee empowerment.

lululemon

 There was a time awhile back when I worked with teams and asked if they knew who the Vancouver-based lululemon was—the men looked confused while the women nodded excitedly. I warned the men to be on the lookout for a clever red bag with positive aspirations such as "friends are more important than money" and "write down two personal, two business, and two health goals for the next 1, 5, and 10 years. Do this four times a year. Goal setting triggers your subconscious computer."

As it turns out, lululemon really believes in this latter practice for its new hires. During orientation, employees are given a "Vision and Goals Worksheet" (which the company shares freely on the internet), and then are encouraged to share with others in their orientation group, as you never know where your resources and support might come from. If you go into a lululemon store, you can sometimes see a wall of these from the store's employees. I asked one of the employees at my local store, who excitedly told me about the process and how her colleagues and the company had supported her dream of going on safari in South Africa.

When I interviewed the folks at Lenati, I heard a lot about the development of an onboarding process that started with bringing people up to speed to start work, and never having new employees jump right into the work; I also heard good things about how they work with people to get their careers on board, too. They assign everyone a career mentor who keeps in contact with their managers to see where development is going and what opportunities might come up for that employee to keep being developed. This is onboarding on steroids.

Lenati also does some other onboarding things that work. They organize lunches for new hires. They ease them in and schedule them so they are meeting people and learning. If you want someone to be set up for success, they need context, connection, time, knowledge, and a sense of the culture. All of this is possible, and even probable—if, like Lenati, you create the environment well.

In any organization, onboarding is an opportunity to form, re-form, and improve your organization every single time you hire someone new. You can keep creating a place where people want to work. It's the beginning of your employee's experience and sets the tone. This is your unique, first, and best opportunity to be clear on expectations. Setting people up for success will lead to more engagement later. Bumpy starts, like mine with no desk and chair, can lead to engaged employees but it's hard to get them over that initial misstep.

"Well-managed onboarding programs lead to faster integration, higher productivity, and even delivers better retention."

ABERDEEN GROUP

The Employee Experience Lifecycle

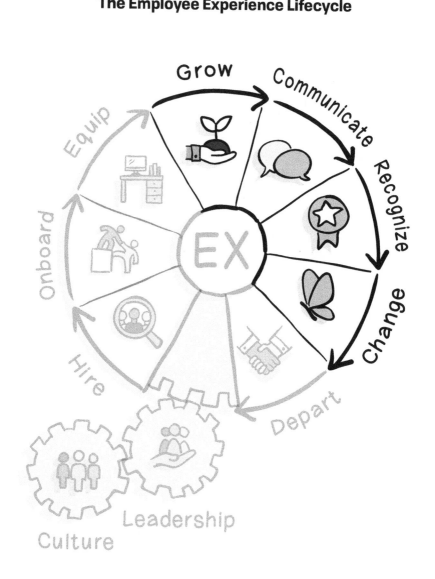

Processes That Enhance the Employee Experience

The Employee Experience Lifecycle

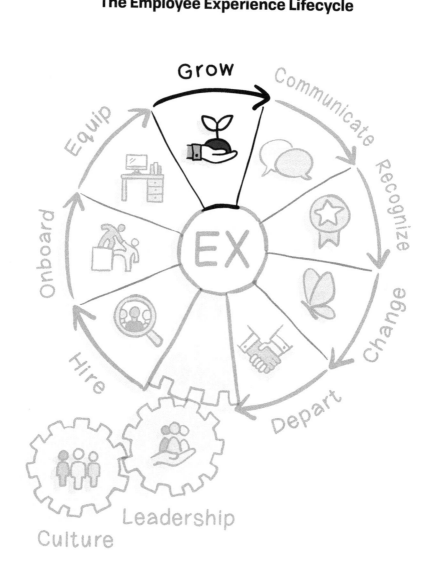

18

Always Learning

MANY COMPANIES FOCUS their efforts on training and development, oftentimes without clear definitions of what is meant by these two terms. As well, many employees seem to be confused.

- **Training** refers to the skills needed to do the job you were hired to do. Many times, people arrive with general skills but need to be trained on specific equipment or processes. Or they know how they do it but not how your company does it.

- **Development** is comprised of skills that make a person more marketable for new responsibilities or positions with your company or elsewhere.

New hires should expect that the company will be training them for their new job. It's in the best interest of the company to make sure that their employees have all the tools, equipment, and knowledge to do their job and perform their best for a company. But who is responsible for development—the company or the individual? And

179

"If you are not willing to learn, no one can help you. If you are determined to learn, no one can stop you."

ZIG ZIGLAR

what is the company's responsibility to encourage and pay for developing people, and what is the payoff?

Caring about people enough to develop them is a form of recognition. We'll talk about recognition in the next chapter. But this is an important point to make here because it distinguishes training—job skills—from development. Development, in my thinking, is a way to say, "I believe in you and your future."

> *"Train people well enough so they can leave. Treat them well enough so they don't want to."* SIR RICHARD BRANSON

This is always a sticking point for me because in one of my early jobs, where I was a training director, I got into repeated conversations where people would say, "Why should I develop someone when they are just going to leave?" And I would say, "I'm developing people so that they become better at what they do. I am creating great people and, yes, it costs money, but in the long run it pays off." What this kind of development communicates is: you care. For the time they work for you, you are making them better people, and this sends a message about how important people are. This is the best kind of conversation, one in which you listen to what they need and you help them get it. You walk the talk.

Fixed Mindset versus Growth Mindset

According to Carol Dweck, author of *Mindset*, there are two possible mindsets that both leaders and employees might have.

Fixed mindset: assumes our character, intelligence, and creative ability are static and can't be changed in any meaningful way. If you have a fixed mindset of yourself, you are always trying to confirm your intelligence, personality, or behavior. Every situation causes you to evaluate:

- Will I succeed or fail?
- Will I look smart or dumb?

- Will I be accepted or rejected?
- Will I feel like a winner or a loser?

If you are a leader with a fixed mindset, you believe that:
- Some people have certain skills, while others don't.
- Each person's learning capacity is permanent and unchanging.
- You can judge someone based on what they have done in the past.
- Past performance predicts future success.

A fixed mindset creates a culture of risk avoidance, as people in this mindset believe they have fixed traits (intelligence, character, and creativity) and what they have are the reasons for success, not the effort put in. This is not a conversation; this is a lecture.

Growth mindset: the belief that what you have is just the starting point for development, and you can cultivate yourself based on effort. A growth mindset thrives on challenge and sees failure as a springboard for growth and stretching current abilities. It assumes that:
- No one has fixed capacities.
- Effective effort stimulates development.

In a fixed mindset you tell people, "I'm not going to bother developing you because you came in with some degree and there isn't any point because you are done, this is it."

With a growth mindset you're saying, "You have unlimited potential and I am exposing you to continuous development because you can always be better and better." If you are doing continuous improvement in your processes, think of it as continuous improvement for your people.

At Lenati, the growth mindset is part of everything they do. Principal Liam O'Connor described it this way:

> One big thing that we're rallying around is the whole notion of growth mindset. If you really distill it down into some of the more

specific behaviors, it's about how we actually model growth as a mindset. It's things like actually celebrating failure, which is challenging across these high-performing consultants who are very nervous about failure, especially when a client is nearby. Or, how we create much more of a learning orientation. We've shifted the whole professional development program from a training program to a learning program. It's a subtle thing, but it's really much more self-driven and it's much less about evaluation across a bunch of tick marks. It's more about having this huge universe of skills and mindsets and things that you can learn and just progressing across those.

My dad, as he got older, set the bar very high for me in terms of continuous learning. He went to UC Berkeley, finished his undergrad there, got into grad school, became a pharmacist, ran his own little pharmacy, and loved it. He then saw the coming of big corporate pharmacies and acknowledged that his job was about to change. Since he didn't want what the future held for pharmacists, he went back to school, law school this time, and became a lawyer.

Even then he didn't stop learning. He took some classes at the local community college, got interested in real estate, and started buying and flipping properties. He learned how to do this so well that he ended up teaching the course he took at the community college.

I recently ran into a student who took a class from him, and the student told me my father taught them some things only a lawyer would know that improved his real estate transactions. His cumulative learning was used for the benefit of his students, not just himself.

My dad then went on to take French classes and history classes, becoming fascinated by ancient history. He was always attending seminars on some subject that interested him. For his whole life he just kept on learning. He modeled being curious through his passion for learning.

Curiosity for learning is a great trait, and one you have to encourage in business environments. For some people, their memories of school are fraught with anxiety and feelings of inadequacy. This may sound odd, but I have found that curiosity can expose them to a kind of work vulnerability that leaders really need to support. You can help them and make it fun and see it as a reward. By sharing new knowledge you can encourage learning and growth.

If you are a leader with a growth mindset, you believe that:

- It's your job to invest in people.
- You need to help people learn and develop.
- Challenges are opportunities to grow and learn, maybe especially from failure.

> *"The only real mistake is one from which we learn nothing."* HENRY FORD

A Growth Mindset Culture

Having a growth mindset culture becomes a powerful support for the organization's capacity to adapt and assures that the organization can survive in an increasingly competitive environment.

A growth mindset creates a passion for learning, while the fixed mindset focuses on a hunger for approval. In the growth mindset, qualities like intelligence and creativity can be cultivated through effort and deliberate practice. In a growth mindset, the view of failure is that we are learning. Those with fixed mindsets see risk and effort as potential demonstrations of their inadequacies. With a growth mindset there's a confidence that you can learn and, through effort, develop your skills and abilities.

By instilling a concept of lifelong learning and providing opportunities for people to learn by doing, you are demonstrating a growth mindset. Research has shown that learning, and feeling like someone cares about your development, contributes to well-being. Most people do not want to do the same task forever and ever. Instead, people seek experiences at work for growth that will help them with career and talent mobility.

Each industry does this differently and every organization that has a positive employee experience finds their own way of encouraging learning and development.

Conversational Learning

One of my favorite things is a concept called "conversational learning." Unlike traditional methods of learning that place primary emphasis on abstract and conceptual dimensions of knowledge, conversational learning equally values the learner's emotional, sensory, and physical engagement in the learning process.

Conversational learning happens in the context of structured conversation. An instructor gives a guiding question or activity; out of the conversation comes the learning. You learn from each other, not like childhood where you learn only from the teacher.

This was how I structured trainings when I did them as an in-house training director. I would give the participants a topic and let them talk amongst themselves. If you wanted to have managers learn to give better feedback, you may just ask the group, "Talk about feedback situations and the challenges in giving and receiving feedback." And then the group has the conversation. They learn and teach each other as they work their way through the topic.

One of my favorite stories about this comes from a fellow consultant who was asked to do a training at the last moment, on safety procedures for switch operators on the electrical grid, a topic about which she knew nothing. However, the people in the room, the engineers, had a lot of knowledge, and so she set them to work, asking, "What are the safety pitfalls you would warn a newcomer about and what would you tell them to make sure they complied with all the possible safety regulations?" By the end of the day they had created a training manual–sized amount of information and felt like real experts. They had conversations, felt valued for their knowledge, and left with a deep sense of accomplishment, not just a packet of slides.

> *"Name the conversation and then allow people to have that conversation. Then have them share back with a larger group."* PETER BLOCK

There are a variety of ways people can continue to learn.

Stages of Learning

Learning is uncomfortable if you are doing it right, and yet all learning follows some basic stages. Those stages, outlined by Noel Birch back in the 1970s, make up a pattern that applies everywhere from riding a bike to learning how to complete job tasks to parenting for the first time. You might remember that we talked about these phases of learning in Chapter 13.

- **Unconscious incompetence**—you don't even know what you don't know.

- **Conscious incompetence**—wow, I am terrible at this!

- **Conscious competence**—I have to concentrate very hard to do this.

- **Unconscious competence**—I don't even remember how I know how to do this, I just do.

This is the consistent pattern that shows up everywhere. If you pay attention, you'll see it when you're doing something you know how to do really well, like driving. You notice and think, "Wow, I know a few things."

I recently decided to learn how to watercolor paint. Having never taken a single art class, but being fairly creative, I got some watercolor paints, brushes, and watercolor paper. I began to sketch in urban settings, and I had *no idea* what I was doing. I had previously been unconsciously competent, but suddenly I was conscious of how much I didn't know. This is a time many people quit because they don't feel they will ever get better and they feel silly being so incompetent (I certainly did!). But I persisted, learning how to mix colors, getting tips and advice from people, and applying the new knowledge. Slowly I have moved into conscious competence, with the hope that, with lots of practice, I can someday be unconsciously competent—just sitting and painting with joy.

As a leader you need to remember these stages; as a conversational leader, you need to talk about them with your people. Your peers. Your bosses. You need to remind everyone that you value the vulnerability they are demonstrating by taking on development and learning and that you've got their back.

I cannot overstate the importance of learning in organizations. Beyond getting you in and doing the job, encouraging learning says, "I care about you as a human being." As organizations need to become more creative and innovative, the people need to have a learning mindset. So, learning lines up individual goals with organizational goals, and everyone benefits. If you can turn learning into a fun thing, even better. But continuously learning and growing ignites your pilot light and keeps you invested in your job.

 At Zappos, raises are given based on individual effort to learn. There are no annual pay increases; so, unless you make an effort to learn and grow your own skillsets, you stay at the same pay. The company focuses 80 per cent of their training on task-related, company-wide learning, while 20 per cent is up to the individual—you can take a class or create a passion project. Within teams, the leader has a variety of choices for how they want to build a team; once a quarter, teams have many unofficial activities like painting pottery or going to a shooting range.

At Lenati, learning is part of being an employee, from having learning lunches with the whole company, in which anyone can present anything they're knowledgeable about, to having an assigned career advisor who advocates for your growth. My conversations with Lenati got me to throw out the word "training" and replace it with "learning" when it applies to development and skills that are not directly job related. At Lenati, they've created mechanisms to ensure their employees grow holistically, which reminded me how important it is to value both job-related growth and personal growth at work.

Learning and growing is the bottom line to success both personally and for a team or an organization. It makes people feel more human, smarter, more engaged, and it changes the culture of your organization. And, best of all, learning is a kind of reward, which we will talk about in the next chapter.

The Employee Experience Lifecycle

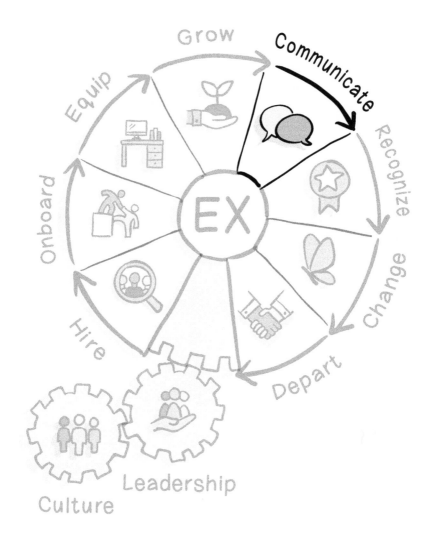

19

Communication Is Vital

OVER THE YEARS, I've worked with groups all around the globe. While there are a variety of issues, one is always consistent: lack of communication. It is impossible to offer a great employee experience without good communication. And let's face it, good communication is a skill we *all* need to develop. Consider that most people are listening to speak, not to hear. When we talked about developing yourself as a leader, we briefly delved into the world of listening, but communication is larger than that—it's a whole way of being that makes or breaks an employee's experience and engagement.

True communication is two-way, whether you are sending an email or hosting a meeting. Communication provides the backbone for all other engagement efforts. It's how you get the right people into the company and working productively. It's how you share the culture of the organization. Most importantly, it's how you build trust. It's the biggest area where things break down, yet it's foundational for everything

Communication isn't a job, it's *the* job. Communication must be wrapped around everything, from the moment someone walks through the door, to day-to-day problem-solving, to organizational

"The biggest problem with communication is the illusion that it has occurred."

GEORGE BERNARD SHAW

changes. It must be predictable, regular, consistent, and repeatable. Some describe it as a cadence, a drumbeat that people can count on. In all the years I've worked with companies, I have *never* heard that there's too much communication—you cannot over-communicate. Maybe some people in our personal lives can say that, but in a work setting, know that more is typically better.

Part of what makes our engagement process successful is that we coach and guide as we communicate—up for the employees and across for the leaders. Everyone begins to understand what their responsibility is in sharing information. So our process helps people begin to listen and hear, speak and be understood in ways that may never have happened before. As I explain the process in the last section of the book, you will see that every aspect of it stresses a different communication skill. At the end of our process, the group has not just solved its issue, the people in the group have developed skills that will carry over to improving everyone's experience.

Talking and listening are both part of communication. A big part of communication is feeling listened to. You can shape the communication so that you appeal to the listener. But you still need to feel heard. And so does the other person.

"Two monologues do not make a dialogue." JEFF DALY

It's safe to say that no one ever felt heard while reading an email blast. Effective communication doesn't mean just shooting off an email. Rather, it means understanding the various ways that you have at your disposal to get messages across, as well as how the audience best receives communication. I've worked with manufacturing facilities where leadership sends off emails, not remembering that most of their employees don't have access to computers most of the day. Efficiency, as in sending a lot of emails or printing lots of documents, isn't the same as effectiveness in getting messages across. Please remember this: email is mostly not communication. It may be a way to share information, but that is not at all the same thing. It has its uses, to be sure, but it is not communication.

> *"The two words information and communication are often used interchangeably, but they signify quite different things. Information is giving out; communication is getting through."* SYDNEY HARRIS

I'm not downplaying the value of receiving information. Sharing information is a great thing. It's something all leaders need to think about. At a senior level, people simply have access to much more information. Senior leaders can decide at their level what to filter in and out. What they forget is that they originally had access to *all* the information, and had the chance to decide what to share. So when very little information gets passed down, and people don't understand or agree, it's often confusing for senior leaders—they can't remember how much they actually know, yet their employees don't have access to the same information. It's a mess. And middle managers seem to get squeezed in this information gap.

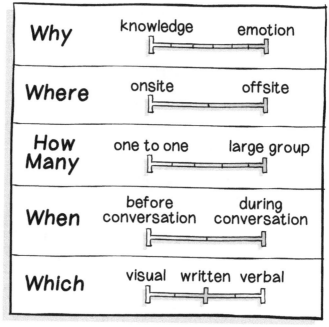

Ways to Communicate

Why	knowledge	emotion
Where	onsite	offsite
How Many	one to one	large group
When	before conversation	during conversation
Which	visual written verbal	

The funnel of communication narrows at every level and tends to break down at the mid-manager level. At this point, the focus shifts to quick dissemination of information rather than effective, quality communication. At this point, the message shifts to bullet points on PowerPoint slides (hint: PowerPoint isn't communication), which lack the "evidence trail" that led to a decision. And, as the communication gets condensed, it becomes a very bad version of the childhood game of Telephone, where the chasm of accurate and useful information going from leadership down to individual employees grows ever deeper.

Then you have just the "what" without the very important "why" as rationale behind it. It's imperative to include the "why"—as Simon Sinek emphasized and which I shared back when we talked about the power of having a clear purpose.

Yvette Huygen, a longtime communication director for global technology and community outreach at Cepheid health care companies, says this: "By talking about 'why' something is being done or was decided, you show employees that you trust and value them, and they are more engaged. This is where many managers fall short, either because they don't grasp the importance of these critical conversations, or they choose not to prioritize the time in their busy schedules."

Unfortunately, the power of the rumor mill in most organizations is strong (it's run by actively disengaged employees) and quickly can spread bad news, misinformation, gossip, and general misery. This negative messaging is very destructive to employee engagement, feeding the actively disengaged and giving them "fuel" to feed to those sitting on the fence.

If you want good communication, take your listener into consideration—what they know, what they don't know, what they need to know, if they feel heard, what they need to understand and have you understand. And guess what? That works best in conversation. Not email or PowerPoint.

I read a story about Steve Jobs, back when he was CEO of both Pixar and Apple. The leadership role was particularly challenging because, while he was spending most of his time at Apple, Jobs

P I X A R

had to quickly assess what was going on when he was at Pixar so he could know where he needed to put his attention. Jobs organized sessions with various teams—the technology team, the *Cars* team—with a dozen in each session. He would then point to someone and say:

Tell me what's not working at Pixar.

After they shared what was going on, he would ask others if they agreed. He would then ask:

Tell me what's working at Pixar.

Jobs would go back and forth with the group until he felt like all the issues were on the table and he had a grasp of what was happening at Pixar. He would run these sessions every few months. And key to his process was to never invite team leaders to these sessions, who would just hinder openness and create a feeling of intimidation. He was smart enough to know he would never have gotten the same level of participation if he'd done this any other way.

Information Is Power

Robert Gaskins, the creator of PowerPoint who then sold it to Microsoft, wrote a retrospective book twenty-five years after the release of his software, and he laments how his creation is being used today. He said back when they invented PowerPoint they were replacing a carousel of slides that had the potential to all fall out on the floor or be put in upside down or backwards. In comparison, PowerPoint is a better technology. But it was never created to take over communication the way it has.

In some Silicon Valley venture capital firms, they will often kick you out if you can't do your pitch without PowerPoint. It has become a complete crutch for communication skills and by using that crutch you lose connection to and passion from your audience. PowerPoint is also *not* conversation. It is not really communication either, unless it is done really well.

I once heard someone say something that stuck with me in terms of inviting people to be part of the conversation: let's try "widening the conversational circle."

What Is Good Communication?

Now that you've heard how not to communicate things through your organization, let's take a minute and discuss what good communication looks and sounds like. This is critical as we've already shown that it's crucial and foundational to creating a great employee experience.

There are so many elements to good communication. When I work with groups, I often feel they are overwhelmed and don't know how to begin. I divide the topic into smaller "chunks" to help better understand where things tend to fall apart and to provide suggestions for improvement:

- Creating space for communication to happen.
- Benefits of good communication.
- The power of good meetings.
- Methods and skills to communicate effectively:
  - across an organization,
  - for leaders with their team,
  - one-on-one.

One example of large-scale good communication is a well-planned conference or meeting. Well-planned conferences widen the conversational circle and allow people to communicate face-to-face. One of my clients worked with one of my favorite leadership coaches, Helen Jane (HJ) Nelson, who prepared the leadership to widen the circle for a conference where they were going to meet with their top 300 people.

All the invited senior leaders learned to share information but also to get their people involved in the conversation. They said what they needed to say and they very consciously and deliberately made their plans transparent to each other. They invited the people one level below them to help chart the future. They concisely shared all the information they had just discussed with their peers and then listened.

HJ's invitation to the leaders, when she works with them, is this: "Collective Dreaming—invite leaders to wholeheartedly embrace the wider system and bring about a powerful collective contribution to your organization." HJ believes, as do I, that allowing more people to be part of the conversation enhances the end product through such an inclusive process.

It's hard to get off the treadmill and think about what things we need to communicate for us to be successful as a team or a business. But it's worth it to stop and think about what you need to communicate and why. As a leader, you have much of the information. When I work with clients, I don't know what needs to be communicated, but, as a process expert, I certainly can help with the *why* and *how*.

Creating Space for Communication to Happen

One Mars client was very passionate about "creating space" in the organization to allow thinking time and communication to happen. He was about creating space in an abstract way, not actual physical space. When you plan an in-person conference, for example, make sure people have downtime to process the information and connect with each other. Or design a workweek where team members have time to think and reflect rather than always doing things.

While it seems obvious, most people run from one thing to another and don't give a lot of thought about what or how they will communicate. Many assumptions are made about what people already know. Creating space is about how you make physical and mental space to create and deliver messages that will be received, understood, and acted upon.

Space can also be viewed as a function of time—allowing ways for people to have conversations that are not tactically oriented, not about "who is doing what by when." This is where innovation and creativity lives, in the spaces between tasks and urgent activities. It's important to consider how to make time for these interactions. Because of time pressures, it's not what we communicate that's the problem, it's what we don't communicate that trips us up.

Modeling the ability to take time away from work to have a life makes it okay for people in your organization to take the time and space they need. You need to have action and activity balanced with time away from the computer if you want your people to do it, too. I had a client recently who told their leaders, "As a leader, if you are sending emails on the weekend or at night, it doesn't matter what your intention is, you are sending a strong message that that is your expectation." And there's information in your behavior that comes across loud and clear. Other people are watching what you do and they hear you. Communication expert Yvette Huygen says, "Most leaders don't think about this. They are just trying to get their work done."

People know who you are and what you are telling them by what you do. It doesn't matter if you say you believe in work-life balance, if you are emailing on a Saturday night, then you are sending a very different message. Be aware that in communication there's the content and then there's this X factor of what you are doing behind that content. That X factor tells a lot.

Creating Human Collisions

 At Zappos, CEO Tony Hsieh encourages "maximum human collisions," where people run into each other and get to know each other in informal ways. When the company moved from Henderson to their downtown Las Vegas space, Zappos purposely created just one entryway so people would have a chance to meet their colleagues. At places like Google and Apple, cafes are designed to be places that

encourage casual interactions and communication between employees within and across teams—about both work and non-work topics.

Space for Good News

There also has to be a conscious and deliberate effort to communicate things that are positive and going well—a "good news" space—as our attention tends to focus on negative rather than positive things. Think about the last time you heard or read good news. Most groups I work with focus entirely on what they haven't accomplished and what's still ahead to accomplish. It's rare that an organization or team will deliberately look for the positives and accomplishments of the team or team members.

Benefits of Good Communication

When people feel like they are connected to the company—the history, the direction it's going, its purpose—they are truly engaged in feeling like what they do matters and they want to help the business be successful.

Even more important, when an employee feels like their direct manager is leading them effectively and cares about them as a person, both in the work that they are doing and helping them to learn and grow, they will want to give their full effort—and that is the very definition of engagement.

Nothing does more to help people feel included, important, and valued than good communication. It's what I have been referring to here as the X factor of communication. It's the way people feel when you have successfully communicated with them, whether it's face-to-face, on the phone, or even through a well-written email.

> *"I've learned that people will forget what you said, people will forget what you did, but people will never forget how you made them feel."* MAYA ANGELOU

I love this quote by Maya Angelou. It simply sums up the idea of the X factor in communication—how you make people feel. I also like it because, like the engagement in an organization, which I started out telling you was a feeling, the same is true of people's unspoken communication. Over time you come to be able to diagnose why their communication, spoken and unspoken, makes you feel the way you do—engaged or disengaged—and what to do about it.

The Power of Good Meetings

Every company has meetings, and everyone at every level attends meetings. Yet in almost every organization I work with, they complain that meetings are the biggest waste of time: inefficient, too many people, no clear purpose.

What people miss is this: internal meetings are probably one of the most powerful tools available to engage people. They are a built-in opportunity to communicate: share information, get input and ideas, coach, support and grow people on a regular basis. I feel so strongly about the opportunities that can be realized through meetings and bigger events like retreats or conferences that I wrote two books about them: *We've Got to START Meeting Like This!* and *To Meet or NOT to Meet?* Both of these books have great tips for organizing and running great meetings and events.

Here are ten tips you can use right now to get your meetings on track.

1. Start by getting organized.

Start with *why*—why are you holding the meeting? Having a purpose is critical. At Sony, you can't book a meeting room if you don't have an objective and an agenda. Then consider the *who* (attendees), *what* (discussion topics), *when* (meeting date and time), and *where* (meeting space).

2. Invite the right people.

Make sure that the people you invite are able to contribute to the agenda and will help move things forward. Don't write a guest list like it's a Hollywood party—it's not. And it frustrates people when they don't know why they're there.

3. Size matters.

Amazon CEO Jeff Bezos says if you can't feed everyone in a team with two pizzas, then you have too many people. The same holds true for meetings. Inviting more people than can effectively hold a discussion leads to diminishing returns.

4. What to talk about.

The agenda should drive the discussion. During the planning process, include a realistic time estimate for each item. It helps to have clear meeting roles—a facilitator to focus on the agenda, a timekeeper to make sure the meeting stays on schedule, and a scribe to write agenda items where everyone can see them.

5. Rules are rules.

Ground rules keep everyone on track. They work best if developed by the group and should be posted so that everyone can see them during the meeting. If it's an ongoing team, it's important to revisit the ground rules until they become ingrained. Rules like *one conversation at a time* and *no technology* help everyone stay focused and engaged.

6. Make it VISIBLE.

Nothing works as effectively to maintain the focus of a meeting as putting information directly in front of people. The idea of a note-taker writing on their pad has become archaic; it's also a surefire way to erode trust and create misunderstandings. It's easy enough to capture ideas and actions on a flipchart or whiteboard, and a variety of apps are available for digitizing and distributing these images.

7. Focus and be brave.

Initially, the meeting facilitator must keep the group focused and on task. Eventually, however, everyone must be willing to demonstrate bravery by pointing out inevitable meeting killers, like allowing the meeting to run long, or not refocusing a participant who has wandered off topic. If agenda items are taking longer than planned, discuss how to handle the situation. Table it? Move other items to a future agenda? Transparency is key.

8. Start on time, end on time.

Imagine if a movie theater restarted their feature film every time someone arrived late. It's important, out of respect to the participants, to start the meeting on time and to end it on schedule. If the meeting ends late, it means the facilitator and timekeeper were not doing their jobs; next time, they need to do better. The whole group shouldn't suffer as a result.

9. Agree who does what by when.

It's important to reserve time at the end of the meeting to visually capture agreed-upon actions. Make sure each task is assigned an owner and an expected delivery date.

10. Check in on how it's going.

Finding out what went well and what could be improved is a great way to model listening and continuous improvement. This way you can make changes for next time that will make the meeting even better.

Retreats and internal conferences are bigger events that can also be used to deliver information and create engagement, learning, and connection. In my research, most people attend events to learn something and network with others. These events have a powerful impact on how people feel about where they work and the people with whom they work. I have worked at conferences where powerful speakers from the outside come and share wisdom that helps to jumpstart creativity. I've also worked at events where the creative, fun team activities help form lasting bonds within the organization.

It's important to create space in these events as well. What forums are available for people to have conversations? How often do you look at a meeting agenda and get tired just thinking about it, or a conference itinerary and wonder when in the world you're supposed to sleep? As a meeting facilitator, I know how to design a productive agenda, so I'm usually shocked at how much is crammed into every minute, sometimes over lunch and into the evening! While on the surface this seems efficient, it's far from effective. People can't process that much content. They need time to talk and discuss things, to refuel their bodies and their minds. Introverts are particularly at risk to be over-whelmed, as they need quiet time to process and recharge their energy.

Yvette Huygen shared a great story about an over-scheduled event: "I attended an intense marketing conference in Nashville where every minute was packed with multiple sessions to choose from. Plus, we were staying in a huge hotel from which there seemed to be no escape. Thankfully, I went with colleagues and we created a game plan: we divided up the sessions we would attend, then gathered at the end of the conference to consolidate our top learnings and take-aways. We had a lively and productive conversation about what we'd learned, impressions of certain speakers, things that excited us, etc. That one conversation gave us a prioritized plan for what ideas and actions to bring back to our company for further discussion. It was incredibly energizing."

Ideas for Communicating Organizationally

Using any of these methods depends on both the purpose and content of the message. It can be a meeting, a conference, a conversation, or some sort of information dissemination, but you need to pick the right mode of communication to achieve your goals. Obviously, if you need input and feedback, a one-way communication tool like a newsletter isn't going to work very well. If you want people to feel engaged in a big group meeting, sharing airtime by having some presentations and some audience interaction is the best combination. These are skills that don't come along with being granted a leadership role in an organization. And often my clients come to me for help because sorting it out is complicated. It's also very, very necessary.

I can tell you from experience, though, you can build leadership trust through transparency. That means sharing both good news and bad news. Sometimes we have to challenge our own views of the "need to know" mentality. Instead of "what to share," you can default to openness. Instead of considering "what not to share," you can think about how to get the most possible input. The best way to build trust is through open communication.

And if you really don't know what works or if what you're doing is effective... ask! I've encouraged many leaders to simply ask their people, "We are doing these things... are they working? What would good communication look like?" If you aren't comfortable doing this in person or are worried people won't be candid, you can start the conversation with a survey; just don't let it end there.

Here are some ways to think about good communication. It's great to follow some of the thinkers in the field, but in the end, just remember that listening to people and telling them the truth in ways that support their growth goes a long way.

Chip Heath and Dan Heath, authors of several books including *Made to Stick*, talk about six principles for creating "sticky messages":

Principle 1. Simplicity—keep it simple and profound.

Principle 2. Unexpectedness—surprise your audience.

Principle 3. Concreteness—use concrete images.

Principle 4. Credibility—allow people to test your ideas for themselves.

Principle 5. Emotions—tap into emotions to convey your point. We're wired to feel things for people, not abstractions.

Principle 6. Stories—tell stories to get people to act on your ideas.

Finding forums to communicate within organizations is important to combat the rumor mill and share with as much transparency as possible. Be sure to think about the *why* behind the *what* and, when useful, who to contact for more information. Here are some great examples of ways to get information out to people:

- TV screens around the building.
- Paycheck inserts.
- Internal websites.
- Newsletters in toilet stalls (at Google, they are cleverly titled "Toilet Times").
- NETMA newsletter ("Nobody Ever Tells Me Anything").

Here are ways to create involvement, allowing employees to be part of the conversation by soliciting questions and getting divergent insights:

- Town Halls or All Hands Meetings.
- Stand-up meetings.
- Gallery walks.
- "IT Happens"—weekly phone calls within IT, where the leader shares current information and takes questions.
- "Safety Wednesday"—a regularly scheduled session to talk specifically about safety.
- Executive trainers—executives teaching pieces of orientation and/or leadership development training (I had senior leaders training in my leadership programs years ago, and it had a significant impact on morale and making leaders feel approachable, as well as giving the leaders insight into what their new leaders were struggling with).
- Skip level meetings—once a quarter at my husband's tech company, he spoke directly with his boss's boss as a means to open communication.

- "Listening Tours"—one of my favorite leaders does these regularly so he can hear directly from employees what's going on and hear about any issues early.
- Public declarations—as a bonus, if you want people to commit to the vision, strategies, and values, there's tremendous power in public declarations, along with writing them down. People tend to be 50 per cent more committed personally when they have written a commitment and shared it publicly. In this way, others hold you accountable for what you have committed to.

Google's TGIFs (Thank Goodness It's Friday)

 Google's TGIFs have been held almost since the very beginning of the company's history. While these hour-long weekly meetings are really held on Thursday afternoon (so their Asian/Pacific counterparts can participate), they are an open forum to hear about company news. The first thirty minutes are led by senior leaders and contain a review of news and product launches, demonstrations of upcoming products, and a celebration of wins. The second thirty minutes are an open forum for Googlers to ask questions directly of the top leaders and other executives about any company issue. Questions range from seemingly trivial topics to ethical concerns.

Besides their weekly TGIFs, Google uses a variety of channels to allow many ways for Googlers to express themselves:

- Allowing Googlers to send direct emails to any company leader.

- Google Moderator allows employees to submit questions, then employees can vote on the topics they are most interested in having answered (note: Google Moderator was one of Google's famous

20 per cent projects—where they allow employees to spend 20 per cent of their workweek on projects that interest them).

- "FixIts" are 24-hour sprints where Googlers drop everything and focus 100 per cent of their energy on solving a specific company problem.

- Employee surveys, where afterward the worst managers receive intense coaching and support; as a result, 75 per cent get better in a quarter.

> *"People look for meaning in their work. People want to know what's happening in their environment. People want to have some ability to shape that environment."* LASZLO BOCK, FORMER SVP OF PEOPLE OPERATIONS, GOOGLE

Zappos Quarterly All Hands Meeting

 Once a quarter, Zappos closes their call center for four hours so they can gather all Zapponians, share company information and numbers, and answer questions. Zappos is serious about these All Hands Meetings: it's a priority for everyone to attend, and all managers commit their teams to attend. The meetings balance things like financial updates with inspiring speakers and stories that connect to the company's mission as well as their fellow Zapponians.

Remember, one of Zappos's values is "create fun and a little weirdness," so there are plenty of quirky touches, such as a kick-off performance of *The Lion King* with employees dressed in animal costumes. It has been described as a high school play mixed with company presentations, along with professional speakers and training workshops, and finishing with happy hour. At this meeting, employees have an opportunity to showcase their talents onstage, whether playing an instrument, dancing, or singing. It may be perceived as all fun and games, but this meeting also has a huge team-building component that requires employees from all departments to collaborate and organize.

Leaders with Their Teams: Giving and Getting Information

Some of the skills needed for a leader to interact with their team are also needed for one-on-one communication. It's important that you are comfortable and understand the value these conversations have in getting things done and engaging people. When you communicate via conversations, people feel listened to and excited—the goal is to create dialogues, not monologues. At Amazon, PowerPoint isn't even allowed in meetings, and meetings are all about conversations.

Having purposeful conversations with people could include questions like:

- How's it going?
- How can I support you?
- What do you need to help you be successful?

It's important also to allow space for pauses. In fact, it's through face-to-face conversations that we reveal ourselves through our pauses and hesitations. It's helpful to use phrases like "I wonder…" and "I'm curious…" to get more information. By initiating conversations this way, issues can be revealed, discussed, and even resolved.

People are hungry for support and direction and for someone to care about their development as people and in their jobs. Think of leading as a way to engage more people: people prefer a "guide on the side," a coach, rather than a "sage on the stage" (what my dad referred to as a know-it-all). If their experience is of being coached and cared about, then truth-telling when things are not going well is more likely.

How to create credible, purposeful communication:
- It's important to project credibility:
  - Strong, articulate voice.
  - Strong posture... stand up straight!
  - Strong eye contact: look for "commas" and phrases to shift focus.
- Be seen as intentional and authentic.
- Your words must match your non-verbals (facial expressions, body language).

If continuous learning is the *doing* part of modeling, then communication is the *being* part of modeling great culture. It's a way of being, not a way of doing. It isn't who I am, but how I work that communicates to people what I want from them, how much I value them, and how much I'm listening to them. If all of those things are present, then I am communicating something that will raise engagement and make people feel more engaged with their jobs, their teams, and their business.

20

Communication and Storytelling

ONE OF THE greatest ways in which organizations are thinking about communications these days is in terms of story and storytelling. Visual and narrative storytelling have always been part of the processes I use: in meetings, conferences, engagement sessions, and how information from these sessions is shared in an organization, so it is great to see the research catch up with what I know from experience. When you read Part Six of this book, you will see how the process I use works. Each step involves turning story to data and data to story through conversations and listening.

My friend and colleague Anthony Weeks, an expert in visual storytelling, talked about how crucial it is to turn data and information into story. We are often "talked to" vis-à-vis PowerPoint decks with lots of data, lots of slides. It's obvious that lots of research has gone into it and you've done your due diligence, but no matter how well it's presented, *who cares* if you can't tell the story about it? Anthony says that, in order to have any impact, there needs to be a balance between data and story. Data is useful, but story makes it stick for

> "Our brains are wired for stories. If we don't hear stories, we make them up."
>
> **BOB JOHANSEN, DISTINGUISHED FELLOW, INSTITUTE FOR THE FUTURE**

people. Story inspires change, data backs up the story. And a visual story is powerful because everyone can see, together, what's going on.

> *"Maybe stories are just data with a soul."* BRENÉ BROWN

These days, there is an obsession with big data; yet, this makes it even more important to be able to distill the information down or you overwhelm people. Good communication, as we talked about in previous chapters, boils down to knowing what is important and choosing how you tell it. In other words, we prioritize what we make time for. It's crucial at the end of presentations to make space to create stories that are repeatable, memorable, and spark further conversations. This is part of great leadership.

> *"Tell me the facts and I'll learn. Tell me the truth and I'll believe. But tell me a story and it will live in my heart forever."*
> NATIVE AMERICAN PROVERB

I have seen this in action over and over when I run my process with clients and I help people to present to each other in ways that are truly engaging. No PowerPoint. No reams of data printed really small on slides. People can learn to do way better than that with a little coaching and motivation.

> *"People only notice stuff that is new and different. You have to tell a story, not give a lecture. You have to hint at the facts, not announce them… because the process of discovery is far more powerful than being told the right answer."* SETH GODIN

Famed storytelling expert Stephen Denning, author of books such as *The Leader's Guide to Storytelling*, shares the reasons leaders need storytelling skills to communicate effectively:

- Sparking action.
- Communicating who you are.
- Transmitting values.
- Fostering collaboration.
- Taming the grapevine.
- Sharing knowledge.
- Leading people into the future

Daniel Goleman is the founder of Emotional Intelligence in the workplace and one of the skills he talks about that is critical for leadership is empathy, as it is a crucial skill for effective storytelling. Anthony Weeks says storytelling engenders empathy because when we embed the story in a personal and human context, we create a bridge between data and emotion through story, and we find out why we should care. Ultimately, a well-told story should make us feel as if the story is happening to us. That is empathy: when we can feel another's experience as keenly as our own.

Storytelling	BusinessSpeak
Captivating	Boring
Conversational	Jargon-y
Outward	Inward
Narrative	Words/numbers
Anecdotal	Mundane
Entertaining	Selling
Compelling	Dull
Real	Staged

Story is how we communicate with each other, and how we bring data to life. It's how we like to be told information, and it's how we listen best. Storytelling is key to engagement because it moves us. Whether you find yourself having to talk about the data generated by an engagement survey, or how we tell the world what a great job an employee did on a project, it can all be done with story. Story sparks all the neurochemicals for connection and attention, so why not use it to up your engagement game?

"Storytelling is about connecting to other people and helping people to see what you see."

MICHAEL MARGOLIS

The Employee Experience Lifecycle

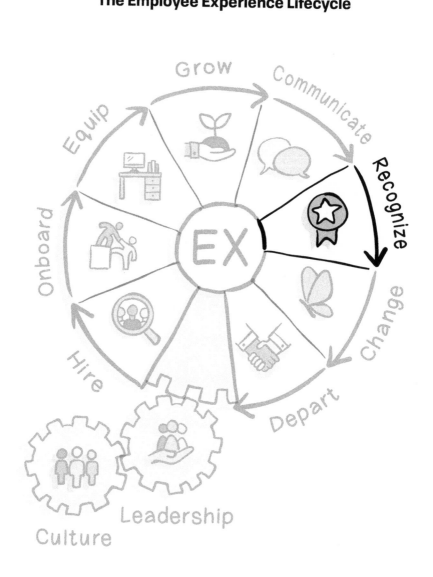

21

Recognition Isn't
about Money

L ET'S FACE IT. With the pace of change and increasing uncertainty
in work and in life, people are craving recognition, acknowledgement, and connection. It's always shocking to me how many
companies don't understand the power of recognition in relation to a
healthy work environment and a good employee experience. Because
of the 24/7 work mentality we've created, it's often impossible to
ever feel a sense of completion or accomplishment. There's always
more to do! As a result, employees often feel disconnected and not
cared about as people. They can feel like they are failing or under-per-
forming, and that sends them down a spiral of misery.

But you can save them, and the solution is simple. Recognize
success when you see it. Call out the behaviors you want to see more
of. Let people know when they have done something well. Reward.
Reward. Reward.

Often, there seems to be a scarcity mentality around recognition,
like there's a finite amount of recognition that is available. This is
simply not true. From my work, I find that the companies with the
best employee experience have recognition built into their culture.

"Brains, like hearts, go where they are appreciated."

ROBERT MCNAMARA

They see what they want to grow in the company and they call it out. They find ways to support their employees' growth by positively reinforcing the skills, behaviors, ideas, and traits they want to see blossom. And it works out for everyone.

Recognition isn't:

- Checking a box.
- Pre-printed thank-yous.
- Recognizing part of a group instead of the whole group.
- Service awards that are sent home in the mail.
- Haphazard, random, and inconsistent.
- Focused on what's wrong or negative.

"Millions of good things are not recognized, yet if you get caught for one mistake, it feels like gotcha." SHARED WITH ME BY AN EMPLOYEE

As Simple as Good Morning. Or Thank You.

In discussing recognition in one listening session, an employee said to me, "It's as simple as just saying 'Good morning.' Or 'Thank you.'" In other words, recognition does not need to be formal to be meaningful. Doug Conant, the former CEO of Campbell Soup, would hand-write and distribute twenty thank-you notes a day to his employees. As long as it's deserved, you can't say "thank you" and "good job" enough. Only 10 per cent of employees say "thank you" to a colleague each day, and only 7 per cent express gratitude to their boss (they say it's lonely at the top). Saying "thank you" demonstrates you care about people and are interested in making a personal connection. It is the first step to a culture of recognition and reward.

One leader said to me, "I wish I could do more, but I have so much on my own plate." I encouraged him to start by thinking of small ways he could recognize those on his team. By doing so, he would build confidence that success didn't have to be big to be meaningful. Even employing the age-old concept of MBWA (management by walking around), leaders get to know people and have a chance to ask about their interests and their families. Humanizing people is an especially good way to create engagement. Once again, it is all about connection and conversation.

What Are the Results You Want?

Companies that are clear on the results they want, and figure out how to recognize achieving those results, are more successful than those that don't. Let me say that again. Companies that recognize the kind of success they want get more success. It's important to make a clear, conscious link with what's being rewarded to the culture you're trying to create.

For example, I've always been amused by companies that give recognition for things like "perfect attendance" and "length of service." While these are nice, what are the unintended consequences of these practices? This drives me nuts. What you're saying is thanks for showing up for thirty years every day even when you were sick and you got us all sick. If you don't pay attention, you'll end up rewarding zombies or creating zombies while the motivated employees with the fabulous ideas go somewhere else where they are noticed for doing something other than showing up.

It's so simple: reward what you want more of. Talk to your people. Find the successes that are already there, and start paying big public attention to them. Those are the building blocks of success.

Determining What's Meaningful to People

You need to determine what people feel is recognition in their eyes. What would be meaningful for people? What are the results you are trying to achieve? Then you design the recognition around that. So, yes, this is another great conversation to have.

To bust a huge myth about recognition, it isn't always money. Money may not be negotiable; even if it is, it isn't always the most motivating force. You need to know your people to know what will motivate them.

At Zappos they give silly things—t-shirts, pins, and other stuff—as a way to recognize achievement. It becomes a thing to have the t-shirt that you can only get through being recognized. But it requires asking people what good recognition would look like and what would be meaningful. You can start the conversation, "Other than money, in what creative ways can we let people know we appreciate them?"

Another Lenati practice is appreciation at quarterly meetings. It began with leaders doing this for the employees and became a way of employees thanking each other for things that went above and beyond. One employee described it as "public recognition of the things we love." This is so healthy that it has grown to be peer driven. That is real success.

Another form of recognition might just be access to the senior folks in an organization. Leaders don't understand that there's a lot of meaning put into having a conversation with them. An email, a thank-you note, or a call means a lot to people who have less access to leaders. If you open up dialogue—even just to say "thank you"—then someone way down the chain of command can say, "I got an email from *the boss*," which opens doors to hearing more, conversing more, learning more.

Recognizing Progress, Not Just Finishing

Even appreciating the routine, day-to-day actions is important to inspire people's best efforts. Teresa Amabile, in her book *The Progress Principle* (co-authored with Steven Kramer), outlines how important it is to recognize people as they make progress, celebrating milestones and achievements along the way. Harder, but still important, is figuring out how to celebrate hard work that happened even if you don't make a goal, like a financial target for a sales team. You can say, "Here were the remarkable things you did. Do more of those for more success next time."

Not everyone likes to be recognized in the same ways, so it's important to determine who enjoys public recognition, versus someone who would be mortified to be recognized publicly and would much more appreciate a private acknowledgement. But don't be fooled by people who say modestly, "Oh, I don't like recognition." *Everyone* likes to be acknowledged for their hard work, creativity, or achievements.

There are formal ways and informal, casual ways to recognize employees. The most important thing to know is it's not really about money. Here are some informal ways to recognize people:

- Ask for people's opinions—people appreciate that you listened.

- Allow employees opportunities to teach or train others informally by sharing knowledge or skills via brown bag lunches or webinars, as well as encouraging them to make presentations at outside conferences.

- Employee spotlight—in venues like newsletters, share what they do at work, their accomplishments, and interests outside work.

- Thank-you notes—as explained, hand-written is better.

- "Day in the Life" opportunities—work side-by-side with a leader or do their job for a day.

- Job rotations or cross-training—chances to learn another job.

- Outside work events—holiday parties, barbecues, and picnics can allow people to interact, especially if families are included.

- Work events—pizza parties or first-day-back catered lunch (after the holidays), for example.

- Fun activities—events, raffles, or contests, which can include company products (e.g., making dioramas out of marshmallows).

- Community projects.

- Baby pictures and family photos—creating a board of employees as babies and asking people to guess who is who, as well as bringing in pictures of employees and their families.

- "Heroes from our community"—find a local hero and bring them into the company, give them a goody bag (possibly with company products or branded items), and make a small donation to their cause.

- Recognition board—posting pictures of people that include their accomplishments.

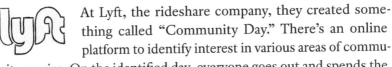 At Lyft, the rideshare company, they created something called "Community Day." There's an online platform to identify interest in various areas of community service. On the identified day, everyone goes out and spends the morning doing community service. In the afternoon, everyone gathers to share what they've learned. You are honoring community commitment and employee insight this way, which is a huge double win.

Bestfoods (Unilever)

One of my most memorable stories about recognition came from my friend and colleague Tom Nerviano, a former client who worked at Unilever for thirty-plus years.

The event was called "Steaks by Staff" served prior to the holidays. About a month prior to the date of the event, flipchart signup sheets are posted in the cafeteria (and the sheets are posted until the day of the event): the name of the servers (leadership team member or management team member, if necessary) with ten slots for each table. It's a bit humbling to see who selects your table and how long it takes to fill the slots. Then the games begin. This is a competition for the highest tips earner by a server; the winner designates (with table input) the charity to receive all the tip money earned by the servers. It's an open competition so your table guests are eager to share their expectations if you want a good tip. And, of course, the competitors downplay or share little of their plans.

The essential meal (steak, potato, salad, packaged rolls, sheet cake slices) and table setting (paper table cloth, plastic utensils, plastic serving spoons, paper plates/bowls, paper napkins, and plastic cups) are provided by the company. We served on all three shifts. The server could do anything to embellish the meal: setup (linens, fine china, silverware, stemware, centerpiece, heated serving equipment, serving utensils), attire (suit, tuxedo, leftover Halloween costume, gown, etc.), meal enhancer (appetizers, special breads, sauces, condiments, side dishes, desserts), beverages (sparkling apple/grape juice, sparkling water, soda, tea, special coffees), and whatever else you wanted to do. The kitchen staff consists of the remaining members of the management team who would prepare the meal, help with cleanup, and support the servers.

The day of the event is great fun. Certainly extremes: next to an over-the-top embellished table (a spectacle) is Fred's table where the guests are served the basic package with a server-tossed (in the air) baked potato and an Entenmann's apple pie cut personally by Fred with a plastic knife.

It was a great way to end the year and say "thanks." In retrospect, it was not costly as we did all the planning, ordered and picked up all the food, cooked, and served our guests. The team members enjoyed being served by "a boss" and had no problem making special service requests. It was something we did together as a management team, we raised money, and we had fun.

 Zappos pays attention to recognition using several programs they have developed. They are true to their core value "Do More with Less" in being scalable and affordable:

1. New Employee Scavenger Hunt—after completing the mandatory month-long training, new hires are assigned challenges to find employees around the company. For example, find someone with a Zappos shirt on and find out how long they have been at the company, or find who schedules training classes and take a picture with them, and find the longest tenured employee in the finance department. Thus Zappos uses the new hires and their acknowledgement of success as a reward.

2. **Zollar Program**—"Zappos dollars" can be earned for participating in training or volunteering to help out. The "dollars" can be used to redeem Zappos-branded schwag like water bottles or gym bags only sold at the company, movie tickets, or Zappos-sponsored charitable donations. The award is accompanied by the reason they are getting the award, which helps make it meaningful.

3. **Master of WOW Parking**—Las Vegas is hot, and covered parking is coveted! Covered parking spots are awarded once a week for a week. Nominations are based on the core value "Deliver WOW through Service" to a co-worker.

4. **Coworker Bonus Program**—a $50 bonus can be given by each Zapponian once per calendar year; managers, supervisors, and team leads are not eligible to receive or issue these.

5. **Hero Award**—in conjunction with the Coworker Bonus Program, this award is given to someone who embraces all of Zappos's core values who is nominated by fellow employees and chosen by leadership. The award comes with a hero cape as well as a $150 Zappos gift card.

6. **Grant-a-Wish Program**—Zappos allows employees to submit and grant wishes, which turns out to be a great way to build a team and family spirit. One inspiring story was an employee who wanted to be a citizen but couldn't afford the fees, which Zappos then paid.

7. **Shadow Sessions**—Zappos allows employees to "shadow" an employee for a few hours to gain an understanding of what they do on a day-to-day basis. This allows people to learn about other people and other parts of the company.

8. Apprenticeships—Employees can apply to become a Z'apprentice even in an area where they may not have previous experience/skills. It allows the employee to check out a new career path and a hiring manager to see if the employee has the right potential to fit the role and team. They have ninety days to try out the role, and it's a mutual decision of whether it's a good fit. If yes, great; if not, they return to their previous role.

Recognition is about making people feel like they're valued and their contributions make a difference. This is part of the definition of engagement, and part of what improves employee experience. People know you put extra effort into actually noticing what they do and that means everyone gets the message about how important they are. Seeing leaders in an actual serving role, for example, makes people feel special. It's beyond noticing they did something; you are saying, "I am going to put the extra effort in because you are important to us as a community." The leader honors the people and shows where the value is. And it makes you feel good, too. You, as a leader, will feel as lit up as the people who get the recognition.

More than that, you grow your organizational capacity for engagement and for business success when you can create the one-two punch of conversation and reward: understand people and find the crossover between what they care about and what your organization cares about.

"Recognition isn't a scarce resource. You can't use it up or run out of it."

SUSAN M. HEATHFIELD

The Employee Experience Lifecycle

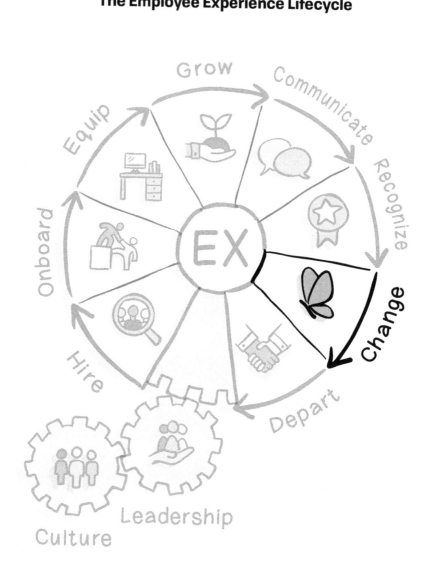

22

Change, Problem-Solving, and Decision-Making

HERE'S NO DOUBT you've heard the term VUCA used in the context of the type of world we live in today: volatile, uncertain, complex, and ambiguous. In other words, change is here to stay and will only get faster. In fact, I've been at many futurist sessions that say the amount of change that will happen in a single day in 2025 will equal all of the changes in the twentieth century.

Of course, people are exhausted from constant changes, shifts in priorities and strategies—this feeling is sometimes referred to as "change fatigue." The terms "do more with less" and "the new…" have become so overused that people often become critical and just wait it out, under the theory that "this too shall pass." Many organizations will tell you that they thrive in a crisis, often described as "firefighting mode," which is another way of saying they are addicted to reacting tactically versus maintaining a strategic focus. In this mode, people are not focused on planning thoughtful solutions.

Aside from firefighters, who wants to sign up for crisis? Are you going to get the right people to take your jobs? Are you going to have

"Never doubt that a small group of thoughtful, committed people can change the world. Indeed, it is the only thing that ever has."

MARGARET MEAD

successful conversations? Are you going to focus on development in the middle of a crisis?

Over-Focusing on the Tactical

Tactical focus is looking at the ground, rather than looking at the horizon, and it does not allow people to focus on the bigger picture. Going back to that cathedral example: if people are being tactical, they are focused on the grout in the tiles, not the cathedral. It becomes mind numbing.

Being tactical all the time also activates that horrible "I'm so busy" response, which keeps you in adrenaline mode for the short-term issue. But if you operate that way on a daily basis, you're also severely impacting people's health and well-being. Too much stress and too much "busy" isn't good for our bodies or our minds.

> "'Crazy-busy' is a great armor, it's a great way for numbing. What a lot of us do is that we stay so busy, and so out in front of our life, that the truth of how we're feeling and what we really need can't catch up with us." BRENÉ BROWN

You have to slow down the speed of the treadmill because being good in a crisis says you are in crisis all the time, and no one can really work like that for the long run. That is simply not an environment where the employee experience is good.

I have a client whose company is doing very well financially: their stock prices are going up, they're acquiring companies left and right. But my client tells a different story—inside the company, people are burning out because there's just more, more, more. More workload, more work, more crisis. And, not surprisingly, they have an engagement problem. The reward at his company for good work is more work. The leadership has taken away things like offsites to work with teams to create plans, and so they are always on the treadmill. They can't meet to plan for the bigger picture so they are always focusing on the tactical.

Patience and Perseverance

"Be impatient with the actions and patient with the results."
NICOLA LAFRENTZ, HR, BEIERSDORF

Organizations need to keep in mind that change requires clear vision, clear objectives and goals, strategies and measures. It requires conversation. More than ever, change needs to be followed with a demonstration of commitment and perseverance. I will often see organizations try something, and before they've allowed enough time for the changes to settle in, they get impatient as they have not seen results and switch to something different. This is the source of change fatigue; if you talk to your people, you will hear all about it.

Make sure that you're patient with your results. You need to wait to see the outcome, because changing plans over and over is a huge setup for loss of engagement. Consider this scenario: you make a change, get impatient and don't wait for the result, decide nothing happened, and set out to make another change before you have even given the first one a chance to happen. It takes time to see what happens and it's better for your people if you don't jump to the next thing so fast.

Reactions to Change: Fear and Safety

People tend to be on radically different levels of readiness for change. In fact, according to John Medina, author of *Brain Rules*, the brain doesn't care about change; it cares about safety. The brain focuses on loss/loss of control, especially as related to things that are important to the person. Leaders need to be prepared to meet people where they are and help them through changes, including considering where you can give control back. Darwin's theory of motivation is that we will do anything to get a benefit and anything to avoid pain.

What makes change successful is the same thing that makes strategy successful and development successful and every other thing we have talked about thus far: conversation. Talk. When people are afraid, they are experiencing FEAR: False Evidence Appearing Real. For some, it's scary; for others, fear presents possibilities. You can help them through that FEAR through conversation.

> *"All great changes are preceded by chaos."* DEEPAK CHOPRA

Stages of Change

Years ago, William Bridges published books about change that are more relevant today than ever. *Transitions* and *Managing Transitions*, two of his books, included a model of a change curve and how people think and feel during different stages of change. The curve demonstrates the need to let go of past expectations and embrace new possibilities and a new reality. This is an adaption of his original model, which recognizes it's not a perfect curve.

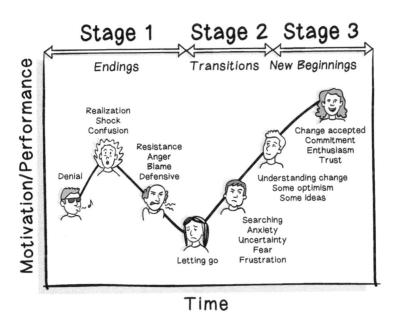

Adapted from an image by William Bridges.

These stages need to be met with appropriate responses to the appropriate groups of people. For example, when a change is introduced, there are generally three types of reactions. There are those who are immediately excited about what's being proposed—"sign me up!" is their reaction. There are those in the middle, whose reaction is "huh?" And then there is the final group of "Negative Nellies," who voice their negativity through expressions like "what a stupid idea!" Typically, managers spend most of their time with this group trying to persuade them why it's a good idea, when actually they should spend the bulk of their time with those who are already on board and excited. Don't forget those early adopters who are ready for change. They are going to be the key to making change stick.

Each of these groups, according to Bridges and to my experience firsthand, need a separate kind of conversation. They will need different kinds of talk and listening, and they need you, as their leader, to be present for the conversations.

"Remember that what gets talked about and how it gets talked about determines what will happen. Or won't happen. And that we succeed or fail, gradually, then suddenly, one conversation at a time." SUSAN SCOTT

During a change process, there isn't anything as important as context-setting conversations. It's important to connect the change to the culture of the organization. When Zappos was going through an acquisition process with Amazon, CEO Tony Hsieh was careful to communicate to the employees what was happening and how it would impact them; as a result, the acquisition was a success.

Change Leadership

"Dialogue is the oxygen of change." RAM CHARAN

The term "change management" is an interesting one: can you truly manage change? Instead, the idea that leaders, with clear vision and strategies, provide change leadership seems more fitting. Having a plan for how the change will happen and being willing to create as much involvement as possible is a better recipe for success. I once heard of a company that did their change management online—you can imagine how successful this was. It was about as successful as an engagement survey with no follow-up.

> *"The secret of change is to focus all of your energy, not on fighting the old, but on building the new."* DAN MILLMAN

Good change allows everyone to be involved, and there are not too many surprises that take people sideways. People feel informed, they know what is going on, they know who to go to if they have questions. It's not too fast, the expectations are clear about what the end will look like, and people identify upfront what success would look like. What does "done" look like? In the final section of the book, I am going to take you through my process for acquisitions and strategy work—and they apply very well to change management—as those are two common types of changes that organizations go through.

Problem-Finding versus Problem-Solving

We often talk about and reward problem-solving, but UCLA professor Iris Firstenberg suggests building in a problem-*finding* approach instead. Meeting with people and asking for their input, including stakeholders, early in the process allows people to be involved and helps spot errors and potential issues. In fact, problem-finding is cheaper than problem-solving because by the time you find errors at the buy-in stage, they are much costlier to fix. By allowing people to be part of the conversation upfront, they can help generate solutions and be engaged in the changes.

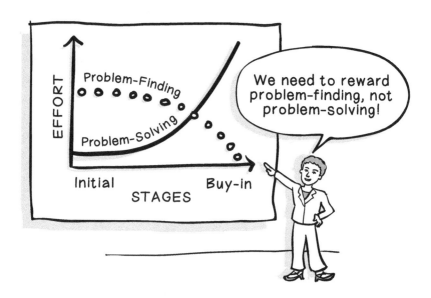

This problem-finding approach is very evident in the design thinking process we discussed earlier on. Firstenberg used as an example the 1992 Los Angeles earthquake, in which a major highway collapsed. The city planners were charged with figuring out what to do about it and how to fix it. The firm that was selected talked to community groups about the repair process and how it would go. They asked the community groups about what problems they anticipated they would have at each stage and the groups helped them figure it out. This gave them ideas about how the problem should be solved and it shared with people what the problem-solving process would look like.

Using this kind of process means that you have to create space to have these conversations and have a pretty good idea of what you are doing. You have to be willing to be curious about what you missed and be vulnerable enough to ask. Listening is a vulnerability exercise. You have to be willing to show your cards and be willing to open yourself up to believe the crowd knows better than you do. The people who work for you know things you don't—and you have to figure out how to learn from them.

How to Encourage Innovation and Creativity

What does creativity have to do with change? A lot of you are going to conduct change through conversation. You want all the best ideas from the entire organization, and you want to use them to create something that works. So, you need to set your people up for success. I use a wide net when I am working with clients and I try to get creative solutions from everyone on every level, sometimes to the extent that I talk to every single employee to find out what they are thinking. You will visit this process in the final section of this book.

People generally get their best ideas and are at their most creative when they have some space to do this, which can include some of the following:

- Time for reflection and analysis.
- Reduced distractions.
- Group inspiration.
- Music.
- Relaxation.
- Meditation.

We are creatures of habit: we see a problem, revert to our habits to find a quick solution, and as a result we make small improvements. However, if you're not clear on what the root problem is in the first place, then you can't be sure that you've solved the right problem. Behind the increased interest and popularity of design thinking is the idea that iterative, empathetic problem-solving can generate solutions that create radical, rather than incremental, improvements. This approach engenders the ability to "fail fast," that is to experiment with solutions in an effort to find the best ones in the process of learning from one's mistakes, while also leveraging the collective knowledge of a team; no one "owns" a solution, but everyone owns the responsibility to identify opportunities for improvement.

"The road to success is paved with stones of failure."
SAID AT A MEETING BY AN EMPLOYEE

Decisions Don't Have to Be Perfect

Making decisions is an important part of the change process. The way changes are implemented involves making decisions. There is an entire field of psychology centered on making decisions: how and why and who and what happens in making decisions. This should alert you to the idea that making decisions is complex and needs to be treated carefully. We all have to do it, so it's not impossible. But it is something to be undertaken with thought and conversation.

The goal in decision-making should be to allow information and ideas to come from everywhere and everyone: participation is encouraged, even expected. Involved people, especially in things that affect them, can help create buy-in and move things forward faster.

Often, organizations use a consensus model for decisions, which means everyone must agree. Sounds good, right? Everyone talking and deciding together? Well, it doesn't play out that way in real life. This practice paralyzes most groups from ever making decisions. Instead, for real conversation to happen, it needs to be okay to challenge. Invite questioning and encourage skepticism, which is different than cynicism. But ask for input and allow disagreement. You can make decisions, try it out, see what happens, take real input, and discuss and change again. At the heart of innovation is the concept of iterations—ideas that are refined and adjusted repeatedly. What's most important for groups to decide is when they have reached "good enough" and can collectively agree to an approach, with dissenters saying they may not agree but can and will support the group's decision.

One way to get out of the trap of making decisions that feel big and scary is to think of decisions as a prototype. Prototyping is a crucial step to design thinking, and it's a way to practice failure in a quick and purposeful way. If you can try different solutions, and find what works and what does not, then you can come up in the end with a much better solution than anything you could do on the first try. Specifically, prototyping is a better means of developing iterative improvements because the act of creating a physical prototype gives a group something to react to; while a user may not be able to specifically say, "I want XYZ," anything you put in front of them is likely to get a reaction and, in turn, give you more to work with.

Tamara Christensen told me, "Prototyping helps you get to the best answer, not the quickest or the easiest. It helps you get to a solution that the users, be they your employees or customers, really need." This is an act of empathy, and one of vulnerability and the willingness to be wrong. It takes conversation and listening, and the ability to demonstrate these through action—it's not about telling someone you've heard them, but rather it's about showing them that you've heard them by incorporating their feedback into subsequent iterations of a solution.

How to Change and Solve Problems

One of the best models I have found over the years is described in a book called *Facilitator's Guide to Participatory Decision-Making* by Sam Kaner. In his model, he describes that the best way to get people to solve problems effectively is to help them see the overall process as well as the natural steps involved. At the beginning of any decision, it's necessary to think about the possibilities for solving it. This requires divergent thinking—getting different perspectives, different ideas, and different ways of creating a solution. But at some point, the group needs to stop generating ideas and start narrowing down the viable solutions. Kaner calls this transition "the groan zone" because it's very hard for groups to make this shift. Having the participatory decision-making model available helps people understand that the struggle is natural and an important part of actually implementing a solution.

It almost doesn't matter what system you use for making decisions and managing change, as long as it includes the following: framing the problem well, listening to your users, prototyping solutions, communicating, and taking feedback like a champ. All of these are opportunities to get people involved, to feel like their input is

PARTICIPATORY DECISION-MAKING

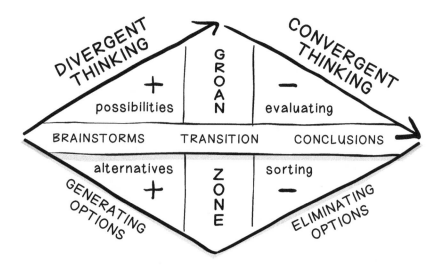

important and their knowledge is useful, and to feel like there's transparency and they know what is going on. When I go in to do engagement processes, I often hear managers say, "I have no idea what is going on. To find out, I have to ask my employees." That isn't okay.

What we are talking about here is change leadership: how to lead thinking and decision-making in ways that improve employee experience and engagement. And it comes down to conversations, but conversations about success. It's important to know how to do this, and what a good process looks like, which we will explore in the next section.

6

Practical Applications

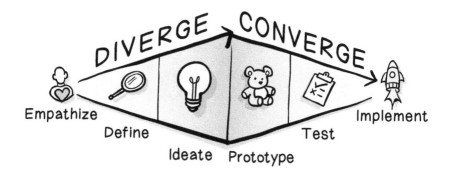

23

Improving Employee Experience Using Design Thinking

DESIGN THINKING, AS we talked about in Chapter 5, is an incredibly powerful way of learning more about an organization's most important customer, their people, and how to use the principles and phases of design thinking to better understand the employee experience and how to improve it. For example, here is a process to think about employees through a design-thinking approach.

1. Create an empathy map
This map will describe your employee's current experience at each stage of their interaction with your company, from the hiring process to becoming an employee.
- How do they see us? What do they see us do with or to them?
- What do they hear from us? What do they hear from others about us?
- How do they think and feel about us?

"As more of our basic needs are met, we increasingly expect sophisticated experiences that are emotionally satisfying and meaningful. These experiences will not be simple products. They will be complex combinations of products, services, spaces, and information. Design thinking is a tool for imagining these experiences, as well as giving them a desirable form."

TIM BROWN, CEO OF IDEO AND AUTHOR OF *CHANGE BY DESIGN*

- What do they say about us?
- What are their hopes? What are their fears?

2. Define their needs and wants

It's important to do some research and find out:
- What makes them feel valued?
- What are their passions, and what do they do to feed them?
- What are their fears, and what do they do to overcome them?
- What challenges them?
- How do they make decisions?

Remember, you are still thinking through their lens, not what you'd like it to be. This phase requires a considerable amount of empathy. As Brené Brown says, "Empathy. We must understand before we judge."

3. Ideate

Spend some time brainstorming ideas for every stage of the employee experience; be creative in your solutions. Look for employees you consider to be highly engaged and get them to help define a great experience. Be willing to also talk with employees who are not so engaged to determine what would create a better experience. More often than not, there are closet visionaries out there just waiting to share their ideas.

4. Build a prototype

Try some experiments on a small scale to see if the ideas work. Select a department or a team that is game to do something different; ask them to write down their thoughts and conclusions.

5. Test

Test your ideas and get feedback from employees, and then start to implement changes one at a time. Figure out how to get feedback so you can make adjustments.

6. Implement

Once you feel like your tests are generating the desired results, roll out the approach to a larger audience, but continue to monitor and adjust.

Using design thinking methodology, you are able to understand and empathize with the employee and create solutions to the problems that are meaningful to them.

24

Team Engagement

ANY ORGANIZATIONS DO some sort of engagement survey, usually annually, to get a sense of how employees are feeling about their work, their team, and the organization overall. As mentioned earlier in the book, the survey results often come back to the organization several weeks to months after the initial survey was taken. There may or may not be a thought-out process for how to bring these numbers back to the teams so they can look at them together and figure out how they can use the results to improve their team.

While you know by now that I'm not a big fan of surveys, I recognize that they are widely used. Therefore, I've designed a straightforward process that can be used with just about any type of team to help take these numbers and turn them into useful information that the entire team can use. While the team leader may be in charge, working together to interpret and then plan changes can build trust and transparency within the team, which in turn improves the employee experience and increases engagement.

First, when the data come back, the team leader should immediately distribute the results, along with scheduling a half-day session for the team to come together and discuss the results. Along with

> "Create the world you
> want to live in."
>
> **ROBIN CHASE, CEO AND
> CO-FOUNDER OF ZIPCAR**

the scores, the team leader should have each team member reflect on the following questions:
- What are my first reactions when I look at the data?
- What have we done, as a team, since the previous survey to improve our team's engagement?
- What are some ways the team leader could help to support my personal engagement to the work, the team, and the organization?

Having team members think about these questions before the session gives them something to focus on in relation to the team, rather than just looking at scores.

The team leader should consider the same questions as the team, and reflect on a few additional questions that will help with the half-day session:
- What do I see as my leadership strengths?
- What are two to three areas I want to improve?
- What are we doing well as a team in each of these areas?
- What are two to three things we could improve as a team?

This is a good time to enlist the aid of HR as a neutral coach and sounding board. After reviewing and reflecting on the survey results and questions, the team leader can meet with HR to express any frustrations, concerns, or questions before working with the team. HR can also be a resource in thinking through the team session.

Once the reflection portion of the meeting with HR is complete, it's time to start thinking about how the half-day session will look. Here are some things to consider for the session:

- How might the team be thinking or feeling about the results?
- As a leader, how do I want to show up in front of my team?
- Who must be at the session?
- Where can the meeting be held that will be conducive to a good conversation?
- What else needs to be considered?

Here are the possible goals for a successful session:

- Having a collective sense of what engagement looks and feels like for our team.
- Understanding the context of the results.
- Agreeing on what we're doing well as a team in six critical engagement areas, and noting where we can improve.
- Creating a team agreement of where to spend energy to make improvements and creating team accountability to make this happen.

There are basically three main conversations that need to happen during this half-day session with the team. These conversations can be facilitated by the leader or a neutral person who is not part of the team, such as an HR representative. The session should start with an overview of the agenda and the goals, and then jump into the main conversations.

Conversation #1: Creating Context—50 min.

It's important to get everyone level-set on where they are with respect to the survey data. Sharing the survey data and questions with the team before the session allows the session to start a baseline conversation with the team.

What was happening around the time that the survey was administered? (For example, there could have been a big organizational change.)

How do we feel about the results and where we are today? (Again, with the time lag between survey administration and results, there may be a change.)

What progress have we made as a team since last year?

Conversation #2: Key Employee Experience Elements—75 min.

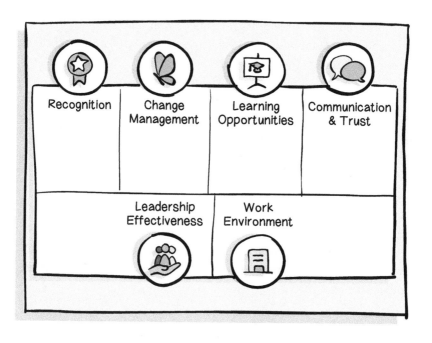

The second conversation in the half-day session looks at six key areas that can affect an employee's experience at work. For each area, consider:

- What are we doing well as a team?
- What do we need to improve?

At the end of this conversation, give each team member two sticky dots and have them place a dot next to items that they feel the team needs to focus on to improve engagement. Tally up the results and agree on two to three items that will have the greatest impact.

Conversation #3: Creating Team Experiments—60 min

For the last part of the half-day session, look at each of the selected items individually, brainstorm a few things that could be done to bring about change, and identify one to two team members who could take the lead. These are called team experiments so there is less pressure to come up with the perfect solution, but instead try some things to bring about positive change. The experiments should be implemented for around ninety days before doing a team check-in to see if positive changes are being seen or to do any troubleshooting that may be needed.

At the end of this conversation, the leader should volunteer one thing they will focus on to do differently in support of the team.

The session can conclude by having each person share how they are feeling about the team and the future, given the important conversations that have taken place.

What is great about this process is that, instead of placing the responsibility solely on the leader to "improve the numbers" or "improve engagement," the team is involved in the conversations and outcomes. As you remember, building trust and transparency, as well as better communication, should be the goal of every leader. This process allows the leader to truly listen to the team and then participate in making changes.

25

Acquisition Engagement

IT SEEMS EVERY day you hear of one company merging with or acquiring another company—sometimes this is to acquire a product, sometimes to enter a new market, and other times it's to expand a skillset or capability. But sadly, mergers and acquisitions (M&A) fail as often as they succeed, often because no consideration was taken for the time and expense of the integration process. While you might be able to align the financials, it's the people who ultimately make a company succeed; without them, you're doomed.

The detailed process that we just walked through together works in many different situations. It definitely improves the employee experience, in both subtle and direct ways. And it's very flexible. In the next two chapters I will take you through two different scenarios where culture can suffer and engagement can be hard to achieve.

One of the key factors to consider is the cultures of the two companies. Remember the quote "Culture eats strategy for breakfast"? It's very true in M&A situations. And, if the culture, along with values and strategy, are not aligned quickly, there's a good chance that the great people will depart and the value will drain from the company.

What makes this situation different is a lot of assumptions are made about how things between the two companies are similar or

"Every single time you make a merger, somebody is losing his identity. And saying something different is just rubbish."

CARLOS GHOSN

different. This happens naturally with every merger or acquisition. The companies are, in fact, legitimately different, and they probably also share some real similarities.

If you don't take constructive steps to address both sets of assumptions, there will be a lot of gossip and watercooler talk about differences when what you want to be having are healthy conversations about differences. So, we use our process to cut right through the misunderstandings.

MARS I have done this kind of upgrade of employee experience with some very big M&A, including the acquisition of Wrigley by Mars, Incorporated in 2008. What stood out for me about clarifying the assumptions in this acquisition was that some of the assumptions on both sides seemed downright silly. We were able to address them in a playful way. This admission of silliness changed the tone of the conversation and allowed us to air even the difficult stuff in a healthy way.

Mars, Incorporated has acquired many businesses over the years in the various segments they operate, be it candy, food, or pet food (most people think they sell only chocolate bars). One of the Mars family members said, "We either love our acquisitions to death or ignore them to death," neither of which was an ideal way to integrate a company.

When Mars acquired Wrigley in 2008, they were determined to do it right. A lot was at stake: as a privately held family business, they don't like owing anyone money; in fact, one of their Five Principles is "freedom," which is about financial freedom from shareholders. But to make this acquisition, they decided to borrow money from Warren Buffett at Berkshire Hathaway. In addition, Wrigley was a company similar in size to Mars, which literally doubled their associate count.

There were several things going in both companies' favor. Both companies had been founded and handed down by family owners. They were started around the turn of the twentieth century and referred to their employees as "associates." They were global companies. Culturally they had much in common from the start.

But, as with any merger, they weren't completely aligned. Mars was one of the very early adopters of an open office concept, whereas

Wrigley status was aligned with private offices; many executive offices were in their landmark building in downtown Chicago. For example, Mars was decentralized in operations and decision-making whereas Wrigley was centralized. There were many other differences, large and small, along with the traditional problem that all companies face: one company had swallowed the other, so one could think "winner" and "loser."

Thankfully, there were a lot of very intelligent people from both companies dedicated to working on the challenges immediately. Mars was determined to make the integration successful. I was fortunate to be brought in to work with the integration team to help design a process that would begin to allow Mars and Wrigley leaders around the globe to learn quickly and ask questions about the other company.

We called the program "Demystifying Mars and Wrigley" and it was run as a four-hour session with leaders in various sites. In the session, we mixed Mars and Wrigley leaders and shared the business reasons for the acquisition and why it made sense for both businesses. We introduced one of the key aspects of the Mars culture, The Five Principles, and allowed the mixed groups to tell stories that demonstrated these principles. Even though they were not the Wrigley values, they were easy enough to create stories from because they were basic ways to interact. The process was designed to help Wrigley associates understand what these values meant in the Mars world and see how their stories also related to The Five Principles.

The Five Principles

1. **Quality**—the consumer is our boss, quality is our work, and value for money is our goal.

2. **Responsibility**—as individuals, we demand total responsibility from ourselves; as associates, we support the responsibilities of others.

3. Mutuality—a mutual benefit is a shared benefit; a shared benefit will endure.

4. Efficiency—we use resources to the full, waste nothing, and do only what we can do best.

5. Freedom—we need freedom to shape our future; we need profit to remain free.

We used wall templates for various parts of the process, and one of my favorite parts of the process was something we called "What's Mad About Mars and Wacky About Wrigley." During this exercise, we had mixed groups of Mars and Wrigley associates sit at tables and talk about the things, in the short time they'd been working together, that were crazy about the other business.

What was brilliant about this exercise was recreating the types of conversations that happen at a watercooler, where people talk about the stupid things that the other company does. But, in this setting, we made it safe and fun to talk about these things, acknowledging that every "family" (in this case, company) has "crazy relatives" (in this case, processes and rules). When the groups would report out, there was often laughter and we would capture these comments on the wall template so people felt their comments were heard.

> *"I think it's really important that people have an opportunity to express what those fears and beliefs are and have an opportunity to create conversation as a way of creating dialogue and human interaction across the two organizations. I believe a lot of culture is translated through stories."* TAMI MAJER, FORMER MARS ASSOCIATE (NOW WITH DANONE)

And now, ten years later, the two companies are a powerhouse in the consumer package goods world; the merger was one of the best Mars ever had. In fact, Tami Majer called the program a cornerstone in the success of the acquisition. She is now working on a similar culture integration project at her new company, Danone, with the acquisition of WhiteWave Foods. She says they're striving to take the best of Danone and the best of WhiteWave, determining what attributes they'll take from each company, based on dialogues with internal teams, to create the future culture of Danone.

Acquisitions can feel different than other kinds of engagement and employee experience issues because they are complicated on so many levels. Often they fail because of cultural differences. So, having a really open conversation about assumptions and culture helps the whole acquisition move forward. While you can't ignore the integrating of systems, technology, finances, and processes, the people part is the most important aspect of an acquisition because it's the people who are making the changes to all those other systems; if they are engaged and on board, then they will do a great job to make the new, larger company successful.

> *"Retaining talent during an acquisition is one of the most critical elements of success. We knew that utilizing the Demystifying Mars and Wrigley program was one of the ways to create an 'Invitation of Belonging' for the Wrigley leaders ... to understand what Mars stood for—so they could make a choice to stay."* MICHELLE THOMAS, GLOBAL INCLUSION AND DIVERSITY LEADER, MARS, INCORPORATED (LEGACY WRIGLEY)

26

Strategy Engagement

THE MAJORITY OF my work over the years has been in vision and strategy development: typically, leaders of an organization or a function hire me to help them figure out their three to five year vision and the strategies that will get them there. In these one- to two-day sessions, we spend a lot of time talking about what's happened in the past, what's in the current environment, and then determining the best ways to move forward.

Just as Acquisition Engagement is a way of getting employees and leaders involved in identifying issues and solving problems, Strategy Engagement helps leaders to work backwards to explain how they came up with the vision and strategies. In this way, the next level of people in the organization can be involved in implementing strategies. Just as with Acquisition Engagement, when you use this process you realize how many assumptions you've made and how much you have already bought into your own ideas. When you need to explain it aloud to people who do not live in your head, you see the gaps in your thinking.

The sessions I run are active and engaging—people are very involved in sharing their views and opinions; they discuss, argue,

> "Hope is not a strategy."
>
> **USAF SPECIAL OPS PILOT**

and finally agree on what's most important. When I'm working with groups, we are capturing all of their thoughts, ideas, and agreements on a series of wall templates.

Regardless of how the process is run, the challenge is at the end. There's a gap between the conversations, discussions, and agreements that come out of these sessions from leaders who are paid to think strategically, and the middle managers and employees who are actually responsible for carrying out these strategies in the organization.

My observation from years of work is this: leaders basically take their vision and strategy and toss it over a brick wall with the hope that the next level in the organization will pick it up and make it happen. What they forget is those well-intentioned people have no context for the ideas—they weren't in the discussions that would help them know why they were doing some things and not others.

The chasm of communication and understanding that's involved in implementation greatly contributes to employee disengagement. When people feel confused or uncertain if what they are doing is making a difference, they lose faith. And sending out a PowerPoint deck or a mass email definitely does not create clarity. Clarity happens through conversations at every level.

We have created several tools to address this gap in understanding in organizations. We developed a series of visual maps that we call "engagement maps," that are accompanied by structured conversations for each map. In this process, when strategy is introduced by leaders, the next level down has a chance to understand and ask questions, which build consensus and agreement to the future direction. Then they are able to truly understand how their work fits into the bigger picture, and they are excited to contribute.

MARS One of the most memorable Strategy Engagement programs I worked on was when the family members of Mars, Incorporated first turned over the day-to-day running of the business to non-family leaders back in 2001. Until then, the company had been led by the two Mars brothers, and business strategies were based on where they wanted to take the company; they had a very hands-on approach to running the business.

With new non-family leaders in place, suddenly the business needed more structure in the way they set the direction for their segments. So we facilitated a session in London, where the "Presidents' Group" discussed and agreed their vision for the business, their business segment strategies, and clarity of roles within the Presidents' Group.

The clock was ticking: they had six weeks until a previously scheduled conference where 140 of the senior leaders from around the globe were to meet. We had to come up with an agenda that would help engage this next level in the work done and help them to communicate within their regions. Challenge accepted!

We worked very hard to design a process and create the materials that would demonstrate the work that had been done and engage these important leaders in the future of the business. For the vision, we designed a process that allowed them to share stories that related to the new vision: Mars, a pioneering family business, passionately engaged, developing leading brands that bring joy to the world. These were broken into six key elements, with questions that could be told as stories. For example:

Pioneer: Share examples of great pioneering spirit at Mars.

Family: How has being a family business made a difference for Mars?

Passion: Give an example of when you've seen passion in others. What do you see? How does it make you feel?

Brands: Share an experience of a brand launch that you are most proud to be associated with.

Joy: What makes you smile about your work?

World: When have we shared ideas to create global wins?

The second part of the conference was dedicated to sharing the global segment strategies and getting feedback from the global team of managers. The segment leaders had to create a presentation that was no more than fifteen minutes, and guess what? They were not allowed to use PowerPoint to convey their strategies, so they had to be creative in their approach. The remainder of the time was spent engaging their audience in discussing the strategies, including collecting their thoughts on what might be missing. We designed table and wall templates and trained some members of the global HR team to be scribes and capture the breakout feedback on the wall templates.

The last part of the conference was a chance for the regional teams to figure out an approach to share the same information. Almost all of the regions decided to follow an identical approach so they could have the same successful outcomes.

Not surprisingly, when you get people involved in understanding the context and big picture, give them the ability to ask questions and understand assumptions, everyone gets on the same page and becomes responsible for their piece of the strategy, turning actions into results. In addition, this process allowed information to flow upward, and the strategies were adjusted and improved based on the feedback that was collected. It's a win for the employees and a win for the organization.

When you take the time to create the process, to work directly on improving the employee experience, you create excitement and buy-in for your strategies. Your implementation path is shortened because people are on board, not just to the *what* you are doing, but the *why* you are doing it. This ties back to Simon Sinek's message about starting with why, which we discussed earlier. It's important to know that everyone who needs to be involved in implementing strategy isn't beginning the process in the same place. If you use this process, then you co-create the starting line and people are excited to be included. Your employees are part of the conversation and they feel the transparency and the honesty about what is going on, helping them see the bigger picture that you see. Better yet, they understand their part in it. To go back to that bricklayer and the cathedral, this process helps everyone understand what cathedral you are building and why their role is important.

ENGAGEMENT BY DESIGN

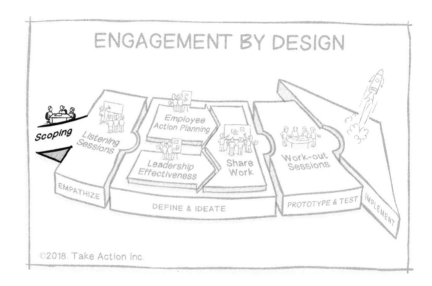

©2018. Take Action Inc.

27

Our Signature Process: Engagement by Design

Step 1: Scoping

As I've said many times throughout this book, the best way to get accurate, reliable information is by actually talking to people. Not by delivering a survey or sending an email where there's no clear understanding of tone or intention, but by creating the times and space where employees can directly express what's going on, share their frustrations and concerns in a safe space. This is a move toward a better employee experience.

I believe that if people knew what to do to create an amazing employee experience, to improve their culture and to create more engagement, they would've already done it. Hence, the need for this chapter and for my work as a consultant. They don't know; they want to know; it's possible to know and to create real and lasting change in any company. The key is being willing to listen.

| *"There are few with power, but many with a voice."* UNKNOWN

What I am going to introduce here is a carefully orchestrated process I use with my clients. We can do it on a huge scale, making sure we touch everyone in an organization, or just part of the organization. I come into organizations to have rich conversations and build and rebuild relationships within the company to help improve the employee's experience and the culture. The process I've created is very customized because, while there can be commonalities when employee experience goes wrong, every situation is unique.

At the beginning of the book I said that surveys are not a healing tool for organizations. People use them with good intention, because it's the easiest thing to do or the most commonly known. A survey gives them information they can compare with other organizations, or within their own organizations over time. But it doesn't actually help fix anything. The real work is in the conversations. A number has no nuance; you can't give empathy to a number and a number cannot grow.

"Engagement surveys measure the temperature, while this process looks at the weather." FELIX POPP, HR BUSINESS PARTNER SUPPLY CHAIN, BEIERSDORF

Let me say that again, because the scale of these processes in a big organization is huge, but the principle is the same. The real work is in the conversations.

How do we go about having conversations on a huge or a more intimate scale? We have a process, we plan, and our clients up their leadership game to listen and communicate well. This is a scalable process: I have worked with one HR group or sales group within a company, but have also scaled up the process to an entire site and even many sites over a geographic region.

So, in this first chapter about our process, we will talk about the planning and the preparation—which is the same if you are working with 50 people or 50,000 people.

To do this right, it takes a decent amount of thought, planning, and preparation. And it takes a significant amount of leadership. The process is an investment, both in the business and in the people.

When we do these sessions with big groups, perhaps an entire site, we go in and talk to the leaders first to assess the current situation. What changes have happened recently? How are people feeling about work? What issues could be on people's minds?

We carefully explain how the process works and what we need from the employees and expect from the leaders. We listen carefully to their questions and answer thoughtfully. We collaborate with the leaders to design the process, while sharing what cannot be compromised in terms of the key components we know make the process a success. For example, we have learned you can't shorten the listening sessions to fewer than ninety minutes. And that the action-planning sessions must take place at an offsite location—environment plays a critical role in allowing people to think outside their normal ways of thinking.

We do this for two reasons: 1. To determine if this is the right time to come in with our process, which takes some time to set up and commitment on the back end to deploy—do people have the energy and desire to do this? 2. To assess if the leaders themselves are up for the challenge—are they ready and willing to be open-minded about what they might hear, ready to not take it personally, and ready to help create a different future?

If all of these factors are not there, we don't run the process. Period. It causes more damage to ask people for their concerns and ideas and do nothing than to not start. This is a powerful program that can yield some amazing results, but only if our internal partners are ready to be vulnerable, ready to be challenged, ready to take action.

We've also learned how important good facilitation is. Aside from the leaders, the facilitators can make or break the process. They have to be *"people* people," they need to know how to draw out a group and gain trust quickly. They have to be confident, engaged, and a bit playful. They need to know how to keep conversations at the right level. One of the biggest lessons we've learned is they can't be trainers who expect to have a script and a repeated outcome, because every group is different. Facilitation is more like improv, where you have to respond in the moment.

"Own the Room"

That's what I always tell the facilitators I train.

Show up early. Be prepared. Have all your materials ready to go. Brides and grooms are early for their big day. Speakers show up to check microphones. After all, you never know what might happen.

Our team once showed up at a swanky hotel in North Carolina, where our internal contact had carefully brought all of the materials to the site early so they would be there. But, when we arrived that morning, they were gone. GONE. Not a scrap of our templates, our markers, or our tape. We looked everywhere. Part of our team started getting creative after twenty minutes and looked for onsite materials we could use. Finally, someone checked the dumpsters and was in disbelief that all of our unused materials that had been carefully placed in the room the night before were binned by an hourly night janitor who took "clean the room" to mean "remove everything in it." Had we showed up ten minutes before the participants, we would have been screwed.

Visuals are another critical piece of the process. The visual templates do a couple of important things: more than anything, they make it look like you're doing something meaningful, as opposed to just rolling in a blank flipchart. The templates help keep focus on the topic and they create transparency. There's no scribe somewhere in the room taking their own version of what they think was said—everyone can see what was captured and make corrections. Research shows the power of visual thinking as a way to listen, collaborate, and take action.

Overall, the preparation supports the idea that, if you get people into the same room, having put some time and thought into preparation, you can literally get people on the same page so they are excited to co-create change and be part of the solution. The tools are simply conversations, visuals, and storytelling.

Don't believe me?

I've been designing, refining, and delivering this process around the globe for over ten years. I've seen magic happen over and over, asking employees to share their concerns, sharing the results, and then working to help shape a different future. When leaders hear directly from the employees, they commit to change the way they lead. By allowing everyone to participate, you can make sure all voices are heard.

> *"It's a very visible process—[as leaders, we are] on the hook to do some thing with this information or you lose all credibility."* HR LEADER
> AT A CLIENT SITE

Step 2: Conducting Listening Sessions

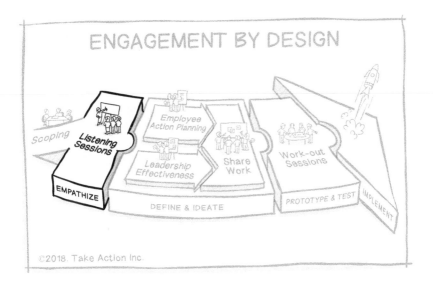

> *"Questions are taken for granted rather than given a starring role in the human drama. Yet all my teaching and consulting experience has taught me that what builds a relationship, what solves problems, what moves things forward is asking the right questions. Humble Inquiry is the fine art of drawing someone out, of asking questions to which you do not already know the answer, of building a relationship based on curiosity and interest in the other person."* EDGAR H. SCHEIN,
> CONSULTANT AND AUTHOR OF *HUMBLE INQUIRY*

The next step in our process is to use the concept of Humble Inquiry to have the first conversations. This can be daunting, but with trained facilitators and visual templates, it's amazing what comes out of the process. People feel heard and great ideas bubble up, identifying both positives as well as where people are having less than stellar employee experiences.

Believe me, people in the trenches know what the issues are; if you set up the environment, they will share. They are the content providers. People want to be heard and have a voice and feel valued when they are asked for their opinion. Consultant Peter Block says you must "issue the invitation" so they can choose to participate, and once they make this choice, they can contribute to making things better and feel like they made a positive contribution.

Facilitators play a valuable role in creating a safe and supportive space for people to speak. The physical space, for example, has an impact—simply removing tables and putting chairs in a semi-circle allows everyone to see each other—there's no hierarchy and I don't let anyone sit in a self-made back row. Changing the seating changes how people interact.

In order to make facilitation simple, we create templates to fill out. Using large templates as a way to capture information creates structure for the conversation and helps keep things on track. There's a lot to say about the importance of visual learning and facilitation when working with groups. Let it suffice to say here that the templates make the process of facilitation much easier to conduct, as well as make the information useful after the conversations. In fact, my former client sums it up this way:

> *"Capturing something on a piece of paper in front of a group objectifies the problem. It puts it out there, so it's no longer inside a person or group but outside and visible. And when the problem is out there, it has its own existence; people are now outside of and separate from the problem. This addresses one of the toughest issues groups face—people hold conflict in. Once it's out there, though, graphically, it's safer. It's been released into the room. It's not my problem or your problem; it's*

our problem. Now we can muster the courage needed to deal with it and work with it objectively." CARLOS VALDES-DAPENA, FORMER DIRECTOR OF ORGANIZATION AND GROUP EFFECTIVENESS, MARS, INCORPORATED, AND AUTHOR OF *LESSONS FROM MARS*

Research shows there are six primary areas in which employees typically become disengaged. The templates are organized in a way that the group can see and share information about the six primary areas where research has shown employees become disengaged (we have an "other" category to catch things that don't neatly fit into these six "buckets").

1. Work environment
2. Learning opportunities
3. Communication and trust
4. Recognition
5. Change management
6. Leader effectiveness

We also have a template with a framework for positive input, divided in half. We ask for input on what people like about where they work—what are the good things that make them happy to work there? We also ask for their ideas for improvement.

We record the information that comes up in the group in real time. As the group shares, it's not important who says what (in fact, who said it stays in the room). It's important that the comment is captured accurately—this makes it anonymous but not confidential, because the issues and concerns will be shared to start prioritizing and determining how to start making improvements.

"We don't filter what they said. What you see is what they said."
DANA WRIGHT-WASSON

The power of visuals lies in the fact that there's no fudging of people's actual words. They level the playing field and demonstrate that everyone's voice counts equally and is heard. The very first time I ran this process, I didn't realize I was doing a version of employee engagement or would be running the process in more depth years later. I was simply helping a manager I worked with who asked me to help get to the bottom of his maintenance group's grievances. If there was ever a group that would test you, it was this group. As I stood at the chart to write their concerns, a member of the group said something that had the word "shit"—I don't remember all of what he said, but I do remember the silence as everyone watched to see what I would write.

What did I do?

I did what I had committed to do—I wrote what he said, just as he had said it. It immediately changed the atmosphere of the room, because now we had some trust. They knew I wasn't going to "sanitize" what they said. I was now in it with them. I really wanted to hear what the issues were, and they needed to be brave enough to say the truth of what wasn't working.

> *"This is the first time in thirty years I can now go out to work and not think about all of this."* COMMENT MADE BY AN EMPLOYEE AFTER A LISTENING SESSION

This statement was shared with the facilitators at the end of one listening session, and I remember thinking, *"Wow.* We just spent ninety minutes with this guy, and we helped him release pent-up frustrations and issues that have been bothering him for thirty years... just by simply listening."

In fact, people often come up to us at the end of a listening session and say, "Thank you for listening" or "I felt heard."

If it feels like it would be too hard to hear all the bad things, or you don't want to open up a Pandora's box of issues, consider this: be grateful people are still willing to talk, even if it's negative stuff they are sharing—this means they still care. When people shut down and get quiet, they have given up.

Simon Sinek has moved on from talking about *why* to talking about humanity. Through these listening sessions, we demonstrate respect, listening, and inclusion—all very important components of humanizing others. Being listened to, authentically and without judgment, is a gift.

The listening step can touch any number of people. We have talked to everyone in every factory of a major food company or just one HR team. The process is the same. We facilitate the conversation, use the templates, gather what we heard, and make sure what they really said made it on the templates.

> *"Vulnerability sounds like truth and feels like courage. Truth and courage aren't always comfortable, but they are never weakness."* BRENÉ BROWN

Step 3: Employee Action Planning

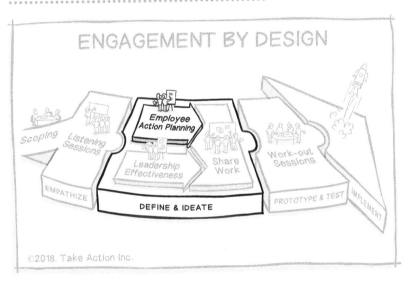

©2018. Take Action Inc.

> *"Be the change you want to see in the world."* MAHATMA GANDHI

What do we do with all the data we collected in the conversations we facilitated? We use them for action planning. We plan with the employees and the leaders separately. Usually, this happens simultaneously with a facilitator and scribe working with employees in one room and another facilitator and scribe team in a separate room with the leaders.

We do this action planning separately with the employees and the leaders to instill confidence within the employees that what they have to say matters. Often, there are issues around trust, and this time to create their own plan helps support them so they can later speak to their leaders with confidence. The employees may not know how best to present their issues constructively and in a way that leaders can hear them. So, we give them some training on the side. Plus, we help the employees move to problem-solving and solution-building, which is always important. No one wants to hear a report of the problems without potential solutions. As coaches, we know the process gets them from point A to point B so they can determine their own best solutions.

We really want the leaders to hear from the employees, so we meet with them separately to focus on leadership. We want the leaders to hear the issues, too, but they are responsible for digesting and understanding, not solving. We will talk about the leadership process in the next chapter.

The employees gain confidence from being pushed to come up with not just the problems but also the solutions. They step into a leadership role themselves by getting all the data from the listening sessions and finding the themes. From there, they work on creating and prioritizing solutions.

At work, we are faced with two challenges: one, so much data that we struggle to make sense of it; two, time constraints that limit our ability to clearly think about what to do. But there's great value in recognizing the value of "crowdsourcing"—that the wisdom often lies in the heads of many and not the few.

People, by and large, want to make a contribution and feel their work makes a difference. At work, problems are rarely created by one person and often take more than one person to resolve. Transparency of the issues helps people to see what the problem is, as well as the factors that contribute. It's only then that people can begin to create resolutions.

In the employee action-planning process, we have two goals:

1. Ignite passion.
2. Innovate action.

We want people to be passionate about their workplace, their co-workers, and the issues and concerns that they care about. The listening sessions are great because it creates energy and excitement as people get things that are on their mind out on the table and captured accurately and visually. But, the process generates an overwhelming amount of data, some of which are noise, some which are signals of things that need to be considered serious. It's important to be able to sort out the information quickly so the signals can become clear and actions taken.

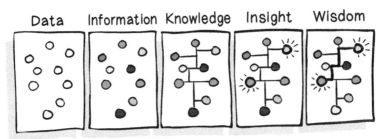

When surveys are done, it can take weeks if not months to get the results. In our process, the data is collected and just a few days later, reviewed, sorted, and prioritized by the people who generated it. The action-planning team represents a cross-section of those who gave input. They are called on to represent everyone and think about what would best serve everyone involved.

> *"Anything that's human is mentionable, and anything that is mention able can be more manageable. When we can talk about our feelings, they become less overwhelming, less upsetting, and less scary. The people we trust with that important talk can help us know that we are not alone."* FRED ROGERS (A.K.A. MR. ROGERS)

The first thing we do is give the action-planning teams all of the raw data, which are digitized versions of the charts that were completed in the focus groups. We don't sort it or type it up because this could appear like there's a pre-ordained outcome. It's important that the group does the hard work of sorting through the data to determine what are the big issues that come up over and over that are on everyone's minds. The power of having the group of employees do this rather than the leaders is that they 1. see how many things are on people's minds; and 2. know what's important.

Once they have sorted and highlighted the insights they have gathered, they are captured again into the six key "buckets" related to engagement (see Part Two). We ask them to narrow these down to the top three to five issues that keep reappearing so there's some level of prioritization. By doing this, we have accomplished a few things:

- We have demonstrated transparency in sharing all of the raw data.
- We have engaged them in the process of sorting and prioritizing the key concerns.
- We have created a level of importance of their role in helping to make change.

This final point is critical, because where surveys leave off is handing the data to leaders to "fix" what's wrong. Leaders often feel they are paid to sort out all the information, figure out problems, and make recommendations and decisions. To some extent, this is true. But in this process, having the employees involved in making sense of the data confirms the right things are the focus of the conversation.

> *"People doing the real work every day know what needs to be done long before the leaders. You need to listen and ask for their ideas."*
> KAT COLE, FORMER PRESIDENT OF CINNABON

Once I had a client who skipped over the employee part and dumped all the feedback to the leaders to sort out. In doing that, the leaders tried to determine who said what and it became a witch hunt. They then tried to dismiss the data once they thought they knew who said it. It was brutal. We learned that you need to give the feedback to the employees so that they can solve it.

This first process is important because it's the first step in helping the participants move from a victim mindset to one that empowers them to create their own reality. People stop having conversations *at* each other and begin to have them *with* each other. They are not the problem, they are the problem-solvers.

Next, we use a different visual process to help make the jump from current reality to a desired future state. We designed a deck of 200 photos, printed on four-by-six-inch postcards, of random, varied things and put them out on the floor. Having just spent quite a bit of time thinking about the issues and concerns that exist today, we ask them to select a photo that represents what working feels like today, based on all of the data they've just shared. These photos are shared "show and tell" style so that everyone can see the picture.

What's interesting about this process, which I have used for many, many years, is that it magically crosses the logical part of people's thinking over to the creative part of people's imagination. I often set this exercise up by saying, "Go with your first instinct; the picture often chooses you rather than the other way around." And then I invite them to tell the story of what the photo they've selected means to them, and it's amazing the powerful stories that emerge from a single photo.

We repeat the process, this time asking people to select a photo that represents what the future would look like if we fixed the concerns they identified. It's a bit like writing a backwards story of success, not the how but instead what it would look like if it were great. This round of the process changes the conversation and the energy in the room. It creates a powerful feeling of *hope.*

The shift in thinking can be likened to stretching a rubber band between your fingers. Remember the story of "creative tension" of vision versus current reality back in Chapter 7? You'll recall that, as you stretch a rubber band, it creates tension and the tendency of the rubber band is to pull back to resolve the tension. Imagine your "vision" is represented by your right hand pulling from above and your "current reality" is represented by your left hand pulling from below. The greater the gap between your vision and reality, the more the rubber band will stretch, the greater tension that will develop, and the stronger the motivation and energy in the system will try to resolve the tension. The goal is to create just enough tension so that you feel pulled along by the vision. If the aspiration is too wild, the rubber band will stretch too far and snap. If it's too conservative, then the rubber band will fall on the table, limp.

I'll never forget one group I worked with, made up of various manufacturing employees of varying genders, ages, races, and educational backgrounds. As with many groups, there were a few gruff, "glass is half empty" employees in the room. When we got to this exercise, one of the burlier men shared his picture, which was of a flower emerging from a rock. He had a heartfelt story about what this picture meant to him that had me, and most of the group, tearing up. He became a total advocate for the great ideas that came up in the group and he was one of the presenters who presented to leadership. What a turnaround.

> *"If we're really going to change, it's going to take everyone."*
> COMMENT MADE BY AN EMPLOYEE DURING ACTION PLANNING

From this point, the energy in the room is electric: we give people choices for the topics they have energy for resolving and they begin to see possibilities. In small teams, the employees generate possible solutions and present them to the larger group; they then vote on the four to five key actions that they feel will make the biggest difference. Limiting the number of ideas creates focus and forces prioritization: "don't try to boil the ocean." As facilitators, we don't direct; instead, we coach them to help generate ideas that will truly make a difference.

The final part of the time we have, preparing to present, is almost as important as what has happened up until this point. Often presentations are given without much thought or planning, but we consider the actual delivery to be key to the success of the process.

For employees, we want them to translate the passion they've had for their hard work over the day into a successful delivery of the results to the leadership. First, we break the day's agenda into components and ask for volunteers to share what happened during that piece of the day, in order of appearance. Then, we coach them on *how* to present. Employees aren't necessarily practiced, skilled presenters, and we want them to be successful. So we take time with each presenter to help them figure out what's important to present (highlights rather than details), encouraging them to share their own story of what was personally meaningful. We identify "props" that can help to convey their message, including the completed visual templates that were generated from their hard work.

It's important to keep in mind that they are presenting not only to their peers and colleagues, but to leaders who influence their work, schedules, and pay. It can be an act of courage to be passionate enough about the work to overcome your own fears of presenting. It can be intimidating to some and a platform for others. We encourage those who are not up front presenting to really be present and supportive of their colleagues, who are representing all of their hard work. It can be deeply moving to watch peers form such a support system so quickly.

I will never forget one session where the employees were presenting their process and ideas to leaders of the organization. One young man got up to do his presentation, and in the middle of talking, he froze. I looked around the room and watched as all of his colleagues leaned forward, some of them whispering, others saying out loud, "You got this!" and "You can do it!" It was like a scene out of a movie. Suddenly, he stood up tall and his voice grew strong and he finished his presentation, followed by a round of applause. The facilitators in the room couldn't make eye contact because we all had been moved to tears by the incredible support we'd just witnessed. The experience reminded us all that we're not alone.

> *"There's not a light at the end of the tunnel, there's a floodlight. We can get this done!"* EMPLOYEE COMMENT AFTER GENERATING ACTIONS TO PRESENT TO LEADERSHIP

I used to describe the employee process by saying there's a point in the day when we cross the "bridge of suicide"—where it just seems so bad and the employees can only see issues. You can get stuck there if you're not careful, but the process is designed with an emotional component because we are trying to compel them to want a change and help create a different future. They get to sit with the juxtaposition between today and the future, and we leave them with it at lunch and they soak in it. They develop the desire to want to be in the future—they are so energized to get to the future. They "cross the bridge" and energetically begin planning solutions. They are excited to share with their leaders.

When I ask the facilitators I work with what the process is like for them, they say how amazing it is to watch the attitudes they see in the listening sessions and the shifts in people's mindsets, from "It's never going to get better" to getting their hands dirty and coming up with solutions and conveying their passion in their presentations. People love the process because it gives them hope. They cross that "bridge of suicide" and come out on the other side, energized by sorting the issues out into priorities and then generating solutions. This is the ultimate employee experience.

Step 4: Leadership Action Planning

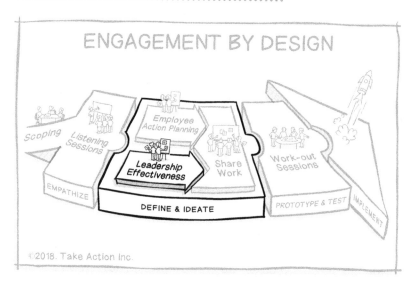

"Now that you know, you can't pretend that you don't." LISA LING

As the employee action-planning group is working, a parallel process is going on with leadership. From the outside, the process looks the same, but the focus is slightly different. We don't want the leaders focusing on competing actions and priorities; instead, we ask them to review the employees' issues and concerns and determine how they can be more effective leaders. It's not a 360 review or a complaint session. In fact, we frame this day as a gift to the leaders—time set aside from day-to-day activities to think, reflect, and plan with the focus on leadership. We use journaling as a way to make the process individual and personal, as every leader is on their own leadership journey, with their individual challenges and learnings.

Of course, we have all the feedback that's been gathered from the employees, and the leaders are anxious to read through it and understand what's being said. Without the well-thought-out engagement process as a framework, this honest feedback could lead to unintended consequences. We often hear "the gift of feedback," yet it doesn't always feel like much of a gift.

"The biggest concern for any organization should be when their most passionate people become quiet." TIM MCCLURE

We are careful to share the feedback in the spirit of making improvements. My colleague Tom reminds them to not take it personally. "It's not about you," meaning the feedback isn't personal, but rather the result of inviting employees—Tom will say "the power of 100 per cent"—to openly share what's on their minds. We encourage the leaders to focus on being curious, looking for signals instead of focusing on the noise. All of the information is simply data to drive improvements. We remind them that pages full of data are better than blank pages, which would indicate people had given up and didn't think it would make a difference.

> *"When you take the time to actually listen, with humility, to what people have to say, it's amazing what you can learn."* GREG MORTENSON, *STONES INTO SCHOOLS: PROMOTING PEACE WITH BOOKS, NOT BOMBS, IN AFGHANISTAN AND PAKISTAN*

We don't let the leaders struggle with the feedback. Instead we guide them to review it at a high level for trends and themes. Most of all, we don't focus on solving the issues, reminding them that there's a room of smart employees who will work on solutions. It's a great opportunity for the leaders to get a pulse of the organization and really learn firsthand the issues and concerns that are on people's minds. We then collect all the feedback and move to thinking about where we go from here rather than starting the blame game.

Shifting the conversation to leadership, we again use the photo postcards to focus in on what it feels like to be a leader. We ask, "What does it feel like to be a leader here today?" Based on the information they've just reviewed, this can lead to quite a candid conversation about the current frustrations. But, while we don't want them to fester in frustration, we do want them to feel that their actions are directly related to how employees feel. Remember, managers are the biggest reason that people leave companies.

The next question changes the conversation: we ask them to think of a leader who personally inspired them, someone current or from their past, someone personal or professional. People share stories of coaches from childhood, parents who overcame hardships, great bosses, and inspiring teachers. The stories are heartfelt and often deeply personal. The stories are used to move the dialogue to one of inspiration and hope. We use the rubber band analogy again to talk about making change and creating a vision.

> *"If you are not being the very best you can be, then you're coasting, which only happens downhill."* DON MILLER

We talk about what the employees need from leaders, and the leaders inevitably know the answers. We ask them, "What are you willing to do differently?" How will they, as leaders, need to work differently in order to help move the organization forward?

They brainstorm, debate, and decide what will be the four or five changes that will move the needle the furthest. We focus on a few things because there's no point in minimizing the impact by doing a little about a lot of things. Instead, it's better to focus on a few leadership topics that are the most important.

What's provocative to me is that a lot of times very basic stuff comes up for the leaders. They want to have the answers, so they're stumped. They ask, "What does communication look like? What do they want? What do I do?"

I remind them: *ask* the employees.

This is a revelation to leaders. They need to get vulnerable and ask some questions to which they don't know the answers. It's really tough not to know the answers. What would good recognition look like? What would good communication look like?

It's okay to say you don't know. It doesn't feel comfortable to ask questions. And yet, asking questions actually builds more engagement.

As with the employees who were preparing to present to them, the final part of this process is to prepare the leaders to present to the employees. Again, we ask for volunteers to present various parts of the day's agenda and outputs. What employees don't realize is that not all leaders are comfortable presenting.

We coach the presenters on both the stories to share and how they present themselves in front of the group. We ask them to sit among the employees when they join the group, be aware of their body language, and smile! It isn't a time to be negative, ask questions, or suggest how things won't work. We coach the entire leadership group about six important qualities they can exhibit during the process and afterward:

1. **Genuine**—show your real self, share your own thoughts and beliefs as a way to build trust and commitment.

2. **Curious**—willingness to listen and seek feedback, being more curious than critical.

3. Vulnerable—willingness to acknowledge that you don't have all the answers, and may need help in resolving issues or problems.

4. Patient—not jumping to solution mode right away, but helping and guiding employees to find meaningful actions.

5. Transparent—sharing information openly and voluntarily rather than hiding it.

6. Gracious—willingness to acknowledge that you don't have all the answers and need help in solving problems and issues.

> *"Listen with curiosity. Speak with honesty. Act with integrity. The greatest problem with communication is we don't listen to understand. We listen to reply. When we listen with curiosity, we don't listen with the intent to reply. We listen for what's behind the words."*
> ROY T. BENNETT, AUTHOR OF *THE LIGHT IN THE HEART*

 The biggest focus for leaders is to demonstrate their openness to listen to the output that will come from the employees—the ideas that they have worked hard to synthesize as areas to work on. I love the GE advertisement "Ideas Are Scary" (you can look it up on YouTube) that shows how new ideas are ugly, messy, fragile—"the natural-born enemy of the way things are." But ideas need to be supported and nurtured, particularly in this setting of building a bridge of trust between leaders and employees who have participated in this process. We prepare the leaders to nurture the ideas and the employees who came up with them.

> *"When people talk, listen completely. Most people never listen."*
> ERNEST HEMINGWAY

Now that both halves of the group are prepared to learn from, listen to, and understand each other, we bring them together to share their work.

Again, put it in the context of the process: what just happened and what comes after?

Step 5: Sharing the Work

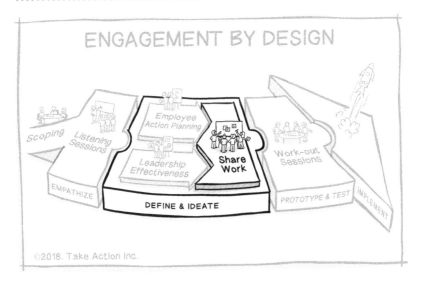

> *"Communication leads to community, that is, to understanding, intimacy, and mutual valuing."* ROLLO MAY

This part of the process is a little bit like trying to have two planes land at the same time on two different but adjacent runways. The employee and leadership processes happen concurrently, so as facilitators, we are trying to calibrate the two sessions so that the parallel processes will conclude at the same time.

The final "act" in the process involves the two groups coming back together and sharing their work, a bit like a "what I did at school today" process. We let the employees share first as a way of recognizing their hard work. We've asked the leaders to be visibly and genuinely supportive of the employees, and we are never let down. Indeed, it's hard to not be excited by the energy the employees put into not only what they present but the enthusiasm in how they present it.

The leaders' work complements and supports the work of the employees, as they share what they know employees need from them as leaders and then share the changes they will undertake as leaders. The two sets of output serve as interlocking puzzle pieces that fit together perfectly.

Both groups feel heard, as the contrast of "what is" and "what could be" are aligned. There's a transformation as the groups enter the process thinking of "us" versus "them" and now there's no sense of "they"—we are all in this together.

The process isn't complete, however, until we do two things:

1. Assign teams to the identified actions—the teams consist of volunteers who are interested and passionate about the topic, as well as at least one leader who can help guide and remove roadblocks.

2. Agree on an action plan to share the output of the process with the rest of the employees who gave input via the listening sessions. This generally involves using the visuals to review the day's process and the outputs in what we call "gallery style" (think of viewing art at a gallery).

There are often people—employees whom the leaders know are troublemakers, and from whom they expect little—who can make a dazzling impression in this process. When people who have been problematic in the past get up and present in an articulate and coherent way, it blows the leaders away. The process the employee has gone through, combined with what they come up with and the coaching they get on how to present, brings out their best self. I have seen it more than once, and it has become my goal to have the leaders blown away.

> *"If you're not part of the solution, you're part of the problem."*
> ELDRIDGE CLEAVER

We then remind people that they are now part of the process, and some people who have not been involved in these sessions won't have had the benefit of the conversations that have occurred and the demonstrations of leadership changes ahead. They may be wary or completely unwilling to accept that things will be different. We remind them that when they go back to work, they need to be aware that negativity feeds on negativity. People who like to gossip and look for what's wrong feed on having an audience. Once they are no longer willing to accept that reality but instead believe things will improve, the negative people lose interest in talking to them because they are no longer feeding their needs.

"Anyone can hide. Facing up to things, working through them, that's what makes you strong." SARAH DESSEN

The final action before disbanding is to ensure that the Action Planning Teams, the five groups who have signed up to work on the five actions, huddle and agree on a first date and time to meet. This is often the most difficult thing to achieve once people leave the room, and we want to make sure they see their group and agree on this crucial first step. We give them an envelope we call the Mission Impossible Packet, which has an agenda and some useful tools for that important first action-planning meeting.

Sometimes we end here and let the groups take it from this point. But in some cases, we move them on to the next phase of the process, which is to start working on the actions.

Step 6: Work-Out Sessions

"When you face a challenge, you can either go through it, go around it, or ignore it." TORY BURCH

As one of my clients said to me once, "It's not going to be enough to talk about what the plan is, we need to wade into the water and start the doing." She was completely correct. It isn't enough to talk

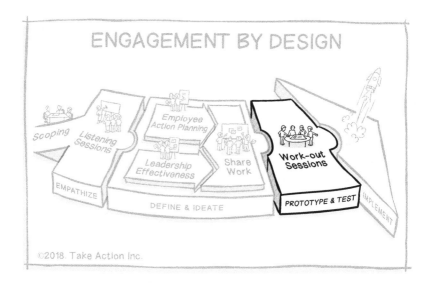

about problems, even to come up with great solutions. People want to see some action.

When we start the work-out sessions, the "doing" part, lots of interesting things happen. There's a relief to moving out of the theoretical. But also, people begin to realize they don't understand the problem as well as they thought, and that it's harder to create changes than they thought. It's vital for employees to know this and feel it—even more important than it is for managers and leaders because often they have some misconceptions about the process.

When I did this process in Thailand, the employees said, "These are our managers' problems, not ours to fix." I thought *this* is why we do the work-out process, because then people learn how complex it can be to resolve issues. So, when the employees said that, I said, "No, everyone needs to work together or nothing will ever change."

Work-out is a process used in Six Sigma to create process improvements. As Jack Welch, former CEO of GE, said, "Trust the people in the organization—the people in the best position to improve a business are the people in the job every day." Work-out, then, is a collaborative process where a group of leaders and employees come to an agreement about what the problem is, using facts and data, not just emotions. All the skills of listening are important. By design, it engages the best thinking of those closest to the issues. Once there is true understanding of the problem, people can focus on what to do.

We've learned that to really help things move forward, we can add a day to begin working on the team's actions. By meeting very soon after the action-planning process has finished, the momentum for change continues. And by keeping the teams together, again using a template and a structured process, the teams are able to have a discussion and create some momentum for their actions. They quickly realize that, if they have selected the right actions, they are complex to resolve—and this is a good lesson for employees to learn. Often employees think that leaders can be counted on to resolve all issues, and often this isn't the case.

The energy of having all the teams in the same room going through the same process with their individual actions is unique. It's like an issue hackathon. The teams, using a single wall template, go through a problem-solving process where they do three things:

1. Describe how things are today and come to a consensus as a team about the problem statement in terms of facts—which can be described as the "As Is" state.

2. Describe what "good" would look like if the problem were resolved—which can be described as the "To Be" state.

3. Create proposals for what needs to happen to get from "A" to "B," and, within that, brainstorm what the options are, and identify the best strategies and actions to resolve the issue.

We borrow some best practices from Google for our process. Google conducted a study of high-performing teams, and one of the important findings was that the best ideas should win in a team, regardless of who puts them forward. The manager or team leader shouldn't have their idea chosen based solely on their role. The work-out process creates a level playing field by having leaders work side by side with employees to come up with plans. And may the best plan win.

 Google also found that psychological safety was the most important factor in high-performing teams. While it's okay to have productive conflict, it must be safe to take interpersonal risks.

In our process, we begin by having each team create a set of ground rules for themselves that they adhere to for the duration of the project. This creates the psychological safety to take the risks necessary for change. Having them to refer back to helps keep it clean.

The first phase each group works on is focusing on the current state—what are the facts of the situation, what has been done, what would someone from the outside see? We are trying to depersonalize it and look at the facts as they are—if I were looking at this as an outsider, what would I see? Have the ground rules set for when people's emotions around an issue start to creep in.

During the second phase, we go over to the goal. This is where lots of groups stumble. They don't fully articulate the end state and can't say when they would know they are fully finished. How will you know that this group has accomplished what they set out to accomplish? Unless you know this, you can't reach the finish line.

The third phase is brainstorming and coming up with a reasonable proposal for actions. What are all the possibilities for making this real? Then we narrow those possibilities to what could actually work. Then we clarify the proposal. Finally, we go step by step to figure out who will do what by when.

At Google, they don't focus on creating the perfect action. Instead, they identify actions to take and call them "experiments," which has the interesting effect of freeing up people to be creative, as they don't feel locked in to finding the perfect solution. In fact, they set up an end date, generally around three months in, where they loop back to assess how things are going and determine if the changes are actually making a difference.

I think of this process as a bridge. Think of the Golden Gate Bridge. In step one you are describing the San Francisco side of the bridge, the second part is the Marin part of the bridge, and the third part is describing the bridge itself.

Then, the teams go work the plan they have come up with. Many teams learn that the problem is much more complicated than they thought, but they wade through the mud and come up with some wins and what they can accomplish. It's encouraging to see how much they take ownership of the problem. They take ownership together; no one walks away and says this is too hard. So even though this isn't their day job, they choose to be here and they become passionate about coming up with solutions.

"I am having employees that were there in the volunteer employee workshop come up to me every day to tell me how the day changed their life—and it was one of the most inspirational days they ever had." TRACY BROCK, FORMER HR BUSINESS PARTNER, UNILEVER

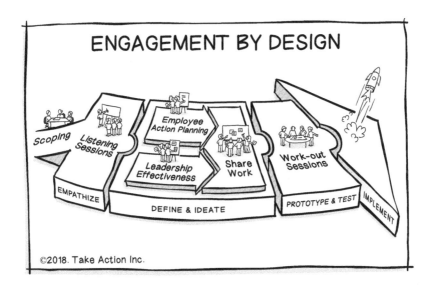

Conclusion

MUST ADMIT, THIS book ended up being different than the book I set out to write, in the best way possible. I'm delighted that so many of the thoughts, ideas, and concepts that I've used in my work over the years have come together here. It's my hope that by going on this journey, you've been reminded of things you may have known or learned in the past. Hopefully you've picked up a number of new ideas and concepts that you can experiment with.

And the key word is "experiment."

Because not everything works for everyone or every place. Some cultures would fully reject the way Zappos operates, for example. And that's fine—not every culture *should* be the same. But the point is to try new things that seem like they could work, perhaps on a small scale. And then check in with people and see how it's going.

The key to creating a healthy organization that people want to join, an organization with a buzz that draws people, is to consciously be aware of the components of a world-class employee experience.

In Part One, I defined employee experience, showed what engagement looks like, and identified how challenging it is to measure these intangible things yet how important it is to figure out ways to capture the hearts and minds of employees. I also shared the basic components of design thinking, which are very useful tools to employ empathy in creating a better experience.

"Act as if what you do makes a difference. It does."

WILLIAM JAMES

"Learning and innovation go hand in hand. The arrogance of success is to think that what you did yesterday will be sufficient for tomorrow." WILLIAM POLLARD

In Part Two, I covered things related to culture—the purpose that the organization declares to the world, the values that employees live by in their work environment, and the vision of where the organization is going. The examples given in this book are proudly shared outside the walls of the organization because companies like Netflix want to make sure that people know what they stand for.

In Part Three, I outlined the components of true leadership—leaders who inspire people to do their best, are willing to be vulnerable, willing to listen, and strive to continuously improve. Organizations who develop these types of leaders and reward them will succeed and inspire a new generation of leaders who understand that their most important job is to take care of their people.

"Before you are a leader, success is all about growing yourself. When you become a leader, success is all about growing others." JACK WELCH

In Parts Four and Five, I discussed how organizations need to recognize that employee engagement is not a survey, but instead is rooted in the experiences an employee has at every stage of their lifecycle within a company. From the hiring process to the day they walk out the door, their experience needs to be positive and productive. Thinking about each step through an employee lens is critical to continuously improving the employee journey.

In Part Six, I shared some of the practical ways you can begin to apply some of this knowledge; it's up to you to determine what things you can do to improve yourself, your people, and the organization. Every little action can make a difference and builds on the previous action.

So what will *you* do?

We often end our Engagement by Design sessions by asking each person to share one word of how they are feeling at the end of the day, after doing the hard work of sorting out the myriad of issues, identifying the key areas to create change, brainstorming potential solutions, and then sharing with their leadership team. This "one word" process is powerful, and sometimes less is more—having to narrow down your feelings to one word that is the essence of how you're feeling is very powerful.

I'm often struck by the incredible power of a single word. Here is a word cloud from a typical session; note that the larger the word, the more often it was expressed.

So, as you find yourself at the end of this book, reflecting on what you've read: what is *your* one word?

Making a Difference:
Kylah and the Earthworms

MY DAUGHTER KYLAH has always been an amazing and compassionate animal lover. I will never forget the very rainy day that we arrived home from school when she was about seven. The walkway was filled with earthworms who had been flooded out of their underground homes. Kylah said, "Take this," and handed me her backpack. She had a determined look on her face, so I took her backpack and walked her little sister Allie into the house. I then went back out to see what she was doing.

Kylah was kneeling down, carefully picking up each earthworm and walking it over to the dirt, where she carefully placed it on the ground. Then she went back to the walkway. I said to her, "Kylah! It's pouring rain out here! You're going to get soaked. The earthworms will figure out what to do."

But she wasn't listening; she was on a mission. And she kept at her earthworm relocation task for forty-five minutes, until she was sure that each and every earthworm she could see was safely placed back in the dirt. I had a warm towel waiting for her when she came inside, where she had a great look of satisfaction on her face. She may not have been able to save all the earthworms that had come out that day, but she certainly helped all the ones she could see.

Acknowledgements

THOSE WHO KNOW me well know that I have been working on this book for a very, very long time. Maybe a more accurate way to say that would be I have been *thinking* about this book for a very long time, because I've spent more time thinking than actually writing. Thinking and collecting information for this book almost became an additional full-time job.

When I started this book, I had fewer experiences and my perspective was quite different. I have most of the book's many false starts in numerous formats: outlines, tabbed notes in a binder, tables of contents, and actual written chapters spread across several computers and apps, and strewn around my office in dusty "paper cities." I have often thought of gathering it all up and just tossing them—sometimes because I was frustrated I would never write the book at all, and sometimes to challenge myself to see how much of the book lived within my head without notes. But I persisted, and amazingly to someone who was such a concise writer in college that I had to triple-space to get a paper to the right length, I managed to write a full book.

Anyone who tells you that writing a book is easy is lying. This is my third book, and all experience brings you is the raw understanding of what lies ahead. Like childbirth, the pain is the same. I am a good writer; I have always written, since I was a little girl. It could be hereditary: my mother was an excellent writer and actually was an editor for a law firm after college. My daughter is an exceptional writer and editor. But the idea of sitting in a coffee shop, happily typing away, is not how it happens for me. Instead, I have to beat down my inner toddler constantly, who wants to get up and do *anything else* but sit still and write.

And so, with three books under my belt (and co-author of *The Visual Facilitation Field Guide*, 2018), I can say it truly takes a village to write a book. There were so many people silently or loudly cheering the writing process.

From a technical side, my editor and coach, Michelle Auerbach, spent many, many hours on the phone with me, teasing out the stories among the data. She helped create a flow from one chapter to the next, so everything felt like it was supposed to be in this book. She also pulled out tidbits from my interviews and helped tuck them neatly into the right spot. My book coach, David Newman, shared his energy and insights into how to create a book that people want to read. My publishing team from Page Two guided the process from start to finish—co-founder and principal Jesse Finkelstein met me over dinner as I explained my concept, Gabrielle Narsted kept the project on track over many calls and emails, Peter Cocking offered brilliant insights into the design (and was patient in dealing with my strong opinions on this topic), Amanda Lewis applied her attention to the fine details of editing, and Annemarie Tempelman-Kluit made sure we had all the right elements in place to market the book appropriately. I am also so grateful to Marianne Rodgers for making the book's illustrations reflect the playfulness of the way I work.

I am fortunate to be able to think of so many of my clients as friends. As one of my longest client relationships, Mars, Incorporated has provided many incredible opportunities to bring my best self to work, trusting me with important processes alongside incredible people. Sharon Heffelfinger was one of the first people I met at Mars long ago when I was pregnant with my second daughter. Sharon contributed her amazing copy-editing skills to reviewing the manuscript not once but three times, always encouraging me that what I had written was really good and very important. Jennifer Schulte and Jim Brodie were there from the very beginning of the first engagement session we did at Mars, and we had such a good time, it was strange to call it work, except I remember we worked very, very hard. My dear friend and former Unilever client Tom Nerviano also reviewed the content, always making himself available to listen when I was stuck on a topic and allowing me to run things by him to see if they were on track. I knew I could count on him for candid feedback. Tom coined the term "the power of 100 per cent" in relation to making sure every voice was heard. Beiersdorf's Nicola Lafrentz and Felix Popp were great partners as we ran the process in non-English-speaking countries. Sondra Norris helped by providing fresh eyes when mine were worn out. There are countless other clients who provided opportunities to practice what I preach while enabling me to learn from them as well.

Creating a mastermind group of like-minded people was critical to getting outside my way of thinking. I could not be more grateful to the wisdom of Carlos Valdes-Dapena and Heather Martinez, both non-fiction authors and consultants. We continue our sessions, sharing ideas and helping each other get out of our own way. Heather was always willing to share her design wisdom when I had trouble stepping away, while Carlos gave his thoughtful insights graciously.

I have been fortunate to have a "tribe" of friends, many who work visually, as I do. I'm so grateful to Janine Underhill and Emily Shepard, both "partners in crime"—in the trenches with me as we run our engagement process and try to "land two planes at the same time." Nevada Lane is an inspiration as a talented organization development consultant and visual facilitator. Anthony Weeks is a wealth of wisdom around the importance of storytelling. Rachel Smith is a calm spirit that helps me redirect when needed. I treasure all of my friends' wisdom, passion, and commitment to my core value of working with people I enjoy. And my dear friend and colleague Jesse Fewell is a sounding board and a kindred spirit, always adding to my thinking.

To all the clients, speakers, and authors who didn't realize they were feeding my soul, making me think deeply, and helping me connect the dots—a huge thank-you. Sometimes I didn't realize what the puzzle I was assembling looked like. In particular, Adlai Goldberg unknowingly exposed me to the concept of employee experience, and suddenly I had a term for something I'd been doing for years.

To the people who graciously agreed to let me interview them for this book, a big thank-you for sharing your wisdom: Cheryl DeSantis, Tami Majer, Mayor Lester Taylor III, and the incredible leaders at Lenati—Antje Helfrich, Courtney Klein, Liam O'Connor, Eric Smith, Pam Spier, and Charles Tragesser. And for the others who contributed quotes and thoughts: Iris Firstenberg, Yvette Huygen, Nicola Lafrentz, Felix Popp, and Michelle Thomas.

And not least of all, to my family who has supported me through business travel, absences, bad moods, and short tempers, yet loved me anyway—thank you. My daughter Kylah has given me insight into the mind of a Millennial and kept pushing me to look at design thinking processes, helping me to make the now obvious connection between design thinking and my own process. I'm so glad she landed at Lenati, where I've been inspired from afar. My daughter Allie will change the world, as she has changed mine, with her passion for the environment and her commitment to living life on her terms: "YOLO" (you only live once). Both girls have taught me that making the world a better place is more important than ever. And to my husband, Wade, who's been on this book journey through some of the hardest parts, know that I appreciate your love and support beyond words.

Abbreviations

BHAG—big, hairy, audacious goals
CEO—Chief Executive Officer
CFO—Chief Financial Officer
CSR—corporate social responsibility
CX—customer experience
EIT—entrepreneurs-in-training
EX—employee experience
FAQ—frequently asked questions
FOMO—fear of missing out
HR—Human Resources
M&A—mergers and acquisitions
MBWA—management by walking around
MSOD—master's in organization development
NETMA—nobody ever tells me anything
OGSM—Objectives/Goals/Strategies/Measures
PRX—Public Radio Exchange
R&D—research and development
SVP—senior vice president
TBL—triple bottom line
TED—Technology, Education, and Design
TGIF—Thank goodness it's Friday
UCLA—University of California, Los Angeles
UCSD—University of California, San Diego
VP—vice president
VUCA—volatile, uncertain, complex, ambiguous

Further Reading

Books I Reference

- *The Progress Principle* by Teresa Amabile and Steven Kramer
- *Work Rules!* by Laszlo Bock
- *Managing Transitions* by William Bridges
- *Mindset* by Carol Dweck
- *The Apple Experience* by Carmine Gallo
- *Made to Stick* by Chip Heath and Dan Heath
- *Delivering Happiness* by Tony Hsieh
- *Facilitator's Guide to Participatory Decision-Making* by Sam Kaner
- *Essentialism* by Greg McKeown
- *Start with Why* by Simon Sinek
- *Thanks for the Feedback* by Douglas Stone and Sheila Heen
- *The No Asshole Rule* by Robert Sutton
- *Search Inside Yourself* by Chade-Meng Tan
- *The 1 Page Business Strategy* by Marc Van Eck and Ellen Leenhouts

Further Reading on Culture

- *Under New Management* by David Burkus
- *The New Gold Standard* by Joseph A. Michelli
- *Organizational Culture and Leadership* by Edgar H. Schein
- *Building a Magnetic Culture* by Kevin Sheridan
- *Engaged Leadership* by Clint Swindall

Further Reading on Leadership

- *Bringing Out the Best in People* by Aubrey C. Daniels
- *Authentic Leadership* by Bill George
- *True North* by Bill George
- *The Missing Piece in Leadership* by Doug Krug
- *Humble Leadership* by Edgar H. Schein and Peter A. Schein
- *Leaders Eat Last* by Simon Sinek

Further Reading on Employee Experience

- *The Happiness Advantage* by Shawn Achor
- *Engaging the Hearts and Minds of All Your Employees* by Lee J. Colan
- *The Art of Engagement* by Jim Hauden
- *Employees First, Customers Second* by Vineet Nayar
- *Drive* by Daniel Pink
- *Eat Move Sleep* by Tom Rath
- *Wellbeing* by Tom Rath and Jim Harter
- *The First 90 Days* by Michael Watkins
- *Multipliers* by Liz Wiseman with Greg McKeown

Further Reading on Communication

- *Radical Honesty* by Brad Blanton and Marilyn Ferguson
- *The Speed of Trust* by Stephen M. R. Covey
- *Moments of Impact* by Chris Ertel and Lisa Kay Solomon
- *The Art of Explanation* by Lee LeFever
- *Crucial Conversations* by Kerry Patterson, Joseph Grenny, Ron Mcmillan, and Al Switzler
- *Humble Inquiry* by Edgar H. Schein
- *Fierce Conversations* by Susan Scott

Further Reading on Design Thinking

- *Change by Design* by Tim Brown
- *The Design Thinking Playbook* by Larry J. Leifer, Michael Lewrick, and Patrick Link

About the Author

DANA WRIGHT-WASSON IS the founder of Take Action Inc., a global management consulting company that applies visual thinking to strategic planning, employee engagement, and leadership. As a recognized speaker, she shares her thoughts and experiences about these topics using stories and data. Through facilitation and training workshops, she deployed her ground-breaking approach for clients like Unilever, Mars, Incorporated, and Beiersdorf. Dana is the author of two other books, *We've Got to START Meeting Like This!* and *To Meet or NOT to Meet?*, co-author of *The Visual Facilitation Field Guide*, and creator of the Meeting in a Box (MIAB) toolkit. Dedicated to improving the employee experience, she founded the Work Happy Project. Dana has a BA in psychology, an MS in organization development, and is a certified coach through the Coaches Training Institute (CTI). Applying creativity in all facets of work and life is Dana's hallmark. She remains curious about the ways of the world—she has visited thirty-eight countries so far—doing things like taking cooking classes as a way to learn about the local culture. As a proud third-generation San Franciscan, she is happily married with two daughters and two stepsons. To learn more about her consulting, please visit **www.take-action.com**. To see what she's up to in helping to make work a happy place, visit **www.workhappyproject.com**.

CPSIA information can be obtained
at www.ICGtesting.com
Printed in the USA
FSHW010409200219
55784FS